AGENDA FOR SOCIAL JUSTICE: SOLUTIONS FOR 2016

Edited by
Glenn W. Muschert, Brian V. Klocke,
Robert Perrucci, and Jon Shefner

First published in Great Britain in 2016 by

Policy Press
University of Bristol
1-9 Old Park Hill
Bristol
BS2 8BB
UK
t: +44 (0)117 954 5940
pp-info@bristol.ac.uk
www.policypress.co.uk

North America office:
Policy Press
c/o The University of Chicago Press
1427 East 60th Street
Chicago, IL 60637, USA
t: +1 773 702 7700
f: +1 773-702-9756
sales@press.uchicago.edu
www.press.uchicago.edu

British Library Cataloguing in Publication Data
A catalogue record for this book is available from the British Library

Library of Congress Cataloging-in-Publication Data
A catalog record for this book has been requested

ISBN 978-1-4473-3288-6 paperback
ISBN 978-1-4473-3294-7 ePub
ISBN 978-1-4473-3295-4 Mobi

The right of Glenn W. Muschert, Brian V. Klocke, Robert Perrucci, and Jon Shefner to be identified as editors of this work has been asserted by them in accordance with the Copyright, Designs and Patents Act 1988.

Cover design by Policy Press
Front cover: photographs by Brian Klocke
Printed and bound in Great Britain by www.4edge.co.uk

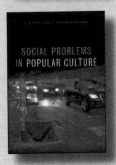

Table of Contents

President's Welcome

David A. Smith

The difference between the Society for the Study of Social Problems and most other academic professional organizations is that for over fifty years, the SSSP has worked to bring excellent scholarship on the pressing issues of the day to agents of change and to apply that knowledge to solutions for those social problems. Our Society's founders really did believe the point was not to simply understand society, but to change it! Today our society is dedicated to nourishing a form of "public sociology" that is designed to be useful to policy makers and activists. It is our way of giving something back to people and institutions that participate in the difficult but essential work of crafting progressive solutions to contemporary social problems. It is in that spirit that we offer the *Agenda for Social Justice: Solutions 2016*. I am very proud to be part of an organization that produces this sort of fine publication and I do believe that it will, indeed, help set the agenda for social justice in the coming years. Thanks to all the authors and particularly the tireless work of Glenn W. Muschert and the SSSP Justice 21 Committee!

Editorial Introduction

Glenn W. Muschert and Brian V. Klocke

> *"The goal of social justice is full and equal participation of all groups in a society that is mutually shaped to meet their needs. Social justice includes a vision of society in which the distribution of resources is equitable and all members are physically and psychologically safe and secure."*
>
> Lee Anne Bell, in *Teaching for Diversity and Social Justice* (2nd Ed.)

The *Agenda for Social Justice* was inspired by the 48th President of the Society for the Study of Social Problems (SSSP), Robert Perrucci. In his 2000 Presidential Address, Professor Perrucci called for a "report to the nation" to be issued every four years, timed to coincide with U.S. Presidential and Congressional elections. These reports, he said, "would be designed to stimulate discussion about 'what we know' [about] the magnitude of existing social problems (e.g., poverty, homelessness, child welfare)," and would propose effective policy solutions to some of the nation's most persistent and pressing social problems. His vision was that such statements would be based on the best research evidence available, but written in language easily consumed by the general public, rather than in academic jargon, with the purpose being "to get people in the wider society thinking about the 'middle range utopias' that could serve as alternatives" to present inequalities.

Not only did Dr. Perrucci speech mark the 50th Annual Meeting of the SSSP, it also helped set an agenda for our work moving into the 21st century. From this inspiration a new committee was formed, the Justice 21 Committee, whose mission is to undertake the challenge set by Dr. Perrucci to contribute to a public sociology of social problems. With the first *Agenda for Social Justice* published in 2004, this one is the fourth edition, and we are pleased to have it published by the Policy Press, whose values align well with SSSP's purpose, "to encourage problem-centered social research and to foster cooperative relations among persons and organizations engaged in the application of scientific sociological findings to the formulation of social policies." Policy Press is an independent not-for-profit publisher, that promotes "the use of research evidence to improve policy making, practice, or social well-being."

Our contributors for this volume come from 14 different public and private universities throughout the United States. This impressive and diverse group of social science researchers and policy analysts consist of graduate students, postdoctoral researchers, and university faculty at all levels: Assistant, Associate, Full, and Emeritus Professors. Among the group are some Endowed Chairs and Directors affiliated with sociology and other social science departments and research institutes. You will find by reading their very brief biographies at the end of each chapter that their experiences include working on President Carter's Atlanta Project, presenting to Congress and state legislatures on economic restructuring, founding a non-profit organization, engaging in community-based social justice action, and many other notable accomplishments. Unfortunately, our limited space does not allow for including a list of the numerous research articles and books written and/ or edited by our contributors, many of whom are extremely prolific.

The first 10 chapters in this year's *Agenda for Social Justice* are contributed by outstanding scholars in their respective areas, and each piece addresses a specific social problem facing the U.S. today. Each chapter can stand on its own, and will certainly be informative in itself. You may also notice that the chapters follow a format that divides the content into three major sections: the first defining the social problem, the second providing evidence available to outline the state of affairs, and the third offering concrete suggestions for the types of policies that would be effective in ameliorating these problems. Each chapter also has a list of key resources for readers to explore more in depth a specific aspect of the subject of the chapter. Chapters 11 and 12, as well as the afterword, are written in a different style and are meant to be think pieces that take a longer and broader view of the mitigation of social problems in general, with an eye toward the pursuit of social justice.

Together these 13 pieces (including the afterword) cover a wide variety of social issues relating to gender, sexuality and injustice; issues of public and environmental health (e.g., food insecurity, health care); injustices related to race/ethnicity, labor, and poverty; criminal injustice; sustainability; the pitfalls of technological determinism; and the importance of social justice movements. We have grouped these chapters into imperfect section titles that give an indication of overlapping and intersecting issues that we hope are useful. It is pertinent to mention to our readers that the *Agenda for Social Justice* is not designed to be an all inclusive list of pressing social problems, for we put out a call for proposals and then select from the pool of submissions received. Noticeably absent from the submissions, for example, were the issues of climate change, police misuse of force, and excessive militarism. Nonetheless, the social issues included are broad-ranging and certainly among the most pressing social justice issues facing the United States today.

It is the Justice 21 Committee's hope that this book as a whole and individual chapters will substantially inform and be useful to students, policy makers, researchers, and the general public. Please take the enclosed research, arguments, and solutions into discussions among your peers, to inspire corrective actions for the social problems in our world, ultimately creating a more inclusive, equitable, democratic, and just society.

Acknowledgements

Though relatively concise, producing this volume would nonetheless have been impossible without the cooperation and support of many good people. We the editors would like to thank our authors first, for working with us and for their quality contributions. It is a pleasure to work with such a group of professionals to bring these ideas to print. We thank our colleagues Patrick Gillham and Jaclyn Schildkraut for their advice on select chapters. As always, we are indebted to Michele Koontz and Héctor Delgado of the SSSP administrative and executive offices, respectively, for their support and encouragement. We thank acquisitions editor Victoria Pittman and her team at Policy Press, with whom we are pleased to collaborate on this book. We thank all the students, scholars, and activists who make the SSSP such an exciting environment in which to study, research, write, and undertake meaningful social action.

Finally, this volume is dedicated to the memory of Professor JoAnn Miller, a founding member of the Justice 21 Committee, who passed away much too soon.

About the Society for the Study of Social Problems

The Society for the Study of Social Problems (the SSSP), is an academic and action-oriented professional association, whose purpose is to promote and protect social science research and teaching about significant social problems in society. Members of the SSSP include students, faculty members at educational institutions, researchers, practitioners, and advocates.

Some of the SSSP's core activities include encouraging rigorous research, nurturing young sociologists, focusing on solutions to the problems of society, fostering cooperative relations between the academic and the policy and/or social action spheres.

If you would like to learn more about joining the SSSP, reading our publications, or attending our annual conference, please visit the SSSP website: www.sssp1.org.

Finally, please consider supporting the SSSP, a nonprofit 501(c) 3 organization which accepts tax deductible contributions both in support of its general operations and for specific purposes. It is possible to donate to the SSSP in general, but it is also possible to donate in support of specific efforts. If you would like to encourage the kind of public sociology represented in this book, please consider supporting the efforts of the Justice 21 Committee. For information on contributing, please visit www.sssp1.org/index.cfm/m/584/.

SECTION I

Gender, Sexuality, and Injustice

ONE

Campus Sexual Assault: Addressing a Systemic Social Problem in the United States

Kristen M. Budd, Alana Van Gundy,
Glenn W. Muschert, and Rose Marie Ward

The Problem

Campus sexual assault is an ongoing social problem that affects public health and public safety in the United States. Sexual assault is a broad term that includes unwanted sexual activity ranging from groping or fondling, to kissing, to attempted or completed rape. Recent surveys estimate that up to 20 percent of female college students and 6 percent of male college students are victims of an attempted or completed sexual assault prior to graduation. Around half of these sexual assaults will happen within the first two years of student's college experience. In general, female college students are more at risk than their male counterparts to become a victim of sexual assault. Female college students are also at greater risk of being sexually assaulted than female non-college students who are traditional college age. In contrast to popular belief, the majority of campus sexual assaults occur between people who know each other. The terms acquaintance sexual assault and acquaintance rape describe this dynamic between perpetrators and victims. Perpetrators use a variety of tactics on their victims including but not limited to threats, coercion, force or threats of force, and legal or illicit substances.

As youth immerse themselves into college culture, unique risk factors such as alcohol use and exposure to particular social contexts such as fraternities and bars increase a student's risk of becoming sexually assaulted. It is estimated that 50 percent of perpetrators, victims, or both are under the influence of alcohol at the time of the sexual assault. The social contexts of Greek life have also been identified as contributing to campus sexual assault. For example,

3

some scholars find associations between fraternity membership and the acceptance of rape myths and or attitudes of sexual aggression toward women. Furthermore, sorority members have been found to be at greater risk than non-sorority members to be sexually assaulted.

The vast majority of sexual assaults are not reported to the police, adding to the difficulty of accurately measuring students' experiences with campus sexual assault. According to research sponsored by the National Institute of Justice (NIJ) that surveyed college students who were victims of sexual assault, 95 percent or more of attempted or completed sexual assaults were not reported to the police. These findings are supported by the National Crime Victimization Survey, which finds that these low rates of reporting by victims have persisted over decades. With regard to campus sexual assault, this lack of reporting may result from a variety of factors such as a lack of student awareness about campus resources; concerns surrounding confidentiality and personal protection; fear of getting in trouble due to campus alcohol and drug policies; fear of negative social reactions from family, peers, or campus authorities; and fear of retaliation from the attacker. Victims have also reported concerns about not being believed by police, being treated in a hostile manner by police or the justice system, or the police doubting the seriousness of the assault. These obstacles exacerbate low levels of reporting campus sexual assault victimizations.

Campus sexual assaults result in a range of consequences, often devastating and life-altering for the victim. These can include psychological distress, such as anxiety, depression, and suicidal thoughts, alcohol and drug abuse, and dropping out of school. Victims of sexual assault often experience symptoms of post-traumatic stress disorder, turn to substance use as a self-coping mechanism, and feel revictimized by individual and system responses to disclosure of the sexual assault. Although leading researchers offer consistent evidence that sexual assault is a potent psychological stressor, campus services and resources are seldom used as students deal with these traumatic experiences.

The Research Evidence

Traditionally, campus sexual assault has been primarily researched from the perspective of the victim and within the framework of heterosexual interactions. As a result, the research evidence presented will reflect this limitation. It is important to stress that lesbian, gay, bisexual, transgender, and queer (hereafter, LGBTQ) college students are also victims of campus sexual assault and we make note of research evidence for LGBTQ college students when possible.

Campus Sexual Assault: Victim Characteristics

- Victims of campus sexual assault are overwhelmingly female college students with male perpetrators.
- Research indicates that sorority members compared to non-sorority members have up to four times the risk to be sexually assaulted during their collegiate career.
- Due to lack of reporting it is difficult to accurately gauge the number of college males who are sexually assaulted. Recent estimates may underrepresent their victimization due to social shaming and stigma associated with reporting.
- LGBTQ students are at similar or increased risk for sexual harassment and assault compared to heterosexual students. For example, the 2015 Association of American Universities study found that 9 percent of LGBTQ students reported being sexually assaulted in comparison to 7 percent of those identifying as female.
- Victims of campus sexual assault are more likely to be revictimized.
- A large portion of college students who are victims of sexual assault use alcohol and other substances as a self-coping mechanism.
- In general, it is estimated that 80 percent of victims of sexual assault experience post-traumatic stress disorder or an ongoing reaction to the trauma. Of relevance to college students, LGBTQ students and racial minority students in particular have greater recovery problems after a sexual assault than heterosexual, Caucasian female students.
- Females who experience campus sexual assault often have a childhood history of sexual abuse.

Campus Sexual Assault: Offender Characteristics

- It is estimated that between 14 and 31 percent of college males perpetrate sexual assault.
- Male perpetrators of sexual assault are more likely than non-perpetrators to have hostile attitudes towards women and to believe rape myths (e.g., women enjoy being raped).

- Research indicates that membership in all-male groups, such as fraternities and athletics teams, is associated with rape-supportive attitudes and self-reported sexually aggressive behavior.
- Male perpetrators of sexual assault are more likely than non-perpetrators to believe in traditional gender roles.
- Male perpetrators of forcible sexual assault are more likely to be repeat offenders. The perpetrator is an acquaintance of the victim in approximately 80-90 percent of sexual assaults; therefore, stranger victimizations in campus sexual assaults are rare. Offenders are primarily current or former significant others, friends, or acquaintances.
- Most perpetrators use verbal coercion and/or intoxication as a sexual assault tactic.
- Men underreport their sexual assault perpetration.

The Role of Alcohol in Campus Sexual Assaults

- It is estimated that alcohol is involved in the vast majority of sexual assaults. Estimates suggest that 50 percent of perpetrators and/or victims were under the influence of alcohol during the sexual assault.
- Both victims and perpetrators of sexual assault report higher levels of alcohol consumption than non-victims and non-perpetrators.
- In social situations, men perceive women who are consuming alcohol, or even just holding an alcoholic drink, as being sexually promiscuous.
- Male perpetrators of sexual assault who used intoxication as a tactic are more likely to practice risky behaviors (e.g., substance use, aggression).
- Victims are more likely to be blamed if they were under the influence of alcohol at the time of the sexual assault.
- Victims of campus sexual assault are more likely than non-victims to report problems with alcohol consumption and post-traumatic stress disorder.

Obstacles to Reporting Campus Sexual Assault

- According to the National Crime Victimization Survey, from 1995 to 2013, only 20 percent of female students reported to police that they had been raped or sexually assaulted. Reasons for not reporting included that it was a personal matter (26 percent), fear of reprisal from the offender (20 percent), that is was not important enough to report (12 percent), not wanting to get the offender in trouble with the law (10 percent), and the police would not or could not help with anything (9 percent).

- According to a U.S. Department of Justice study, victims of campus sexual assault did not report the assault because they felt they would lose social status or be treated like a "social pariah" (42 percent) or because they were unclear on what constitutes sexual assault and if the perpetrator intended to harm them (35 percent). In addition, 70 percent of victims of campus sexual assault reported having no confidence in the university reporting process.
- Victims are concerned to say no or to report assault for fear of organizational retaliation, especially with specific organizational cultures, such as Greek Life, where there is an "implicit expectation of sex."
- Obstacles to reporting same-sex campus sexual assaults are even greater as victims fear additional disbelief and stigma based upon their sexual orientation, social media exposure, and public record disclosures.
- The campus culture regarding campus sexual assault is often viewed as a "culture of indifference," therefore leading students to feel trivialized, unimportant and in fear of additional embarrassment or trauma.
- In general, students and sexual assault victims, who are often emotionally and psychologically distressed, are unaware of where to find (campus) resources and where to go in the time of crisis.
- Victims are often unsure of how much control they will have over campus process and fear additional victimization by using the university (or legal) process.
- Students are unclear if they are afforded any types of protections and or confidentiality in university proceedings. In addition, if students are not redirected to the appropriate offices, such as Student Code of Conduct and/or Disciplinary offices, then their claims may be found to be "unsupported" leading to additional victim shame and guilt.

Recommendations and Solutions

Responses to campus sexual assault must be multi-systemic efforts that include campus administrators and community members, and focus on changing the campus climate. The efforts must work to educate students, first responders, and the general public. Students should have clear guidance on what constitutes sexual assault and "consent," in particular affirmative consent. The role of alcohol and drugs must be a central focus in order to remove the variables that place students at increased risk of victimization. The ultimate goals must include cultivating a campus culture free of victim-shaming, promotion of victim and bystander reporting through an established university process, and the creation of an empathetic and understanding culture that does not make victims feel re-victimized or stigmatized. Recommendations include focusing on continual assessment of campus climate, addressing the role of alcohol in campus sexual assault, reducing obstacles to reporting, and engaging the community in its totality.

1. Continual assessment of prevalence and university policy and practices.

In order to best serve victims of campus sexual assault, it is critical that researchers continue to examine both the prevalence of campus sexual assault, the actual and perceived response by the university, and the existence, efficacy, and reliability of university policy and practices. Therefore, we suggest the following:

- The continuation and validation of campus climate surveys.
- Examinations of the availability of university sexual assault policy and practices, in conjunction with assessing the consistency of university policies and practice.
- The creation of best practices for university responses to sexual assault.
- Consistent measurement of campus sexual assault prevalence that can be compared across colleges and universities.

2. Addressing the role of alcohol in campus sexual assaults.

Alcohol has consistently been found to be a significant contributing factor that increases an individual's risk of becoming the victim of a sexual assault. One critical component of reducing sexual assaults will be to address the alcohol culture on college campuses. This effort must include students, faculty and staff, administration, and the surrounding community, to fully and effectively target the issue. Given that the first few years of college represent a heightened period of experimentation with alcohol, in combination with the higher risk for sexual assault, prevention and intervention efforts should target these time periods. It is a critical time to address student safety and promote education. We suggest the following:

- Reduce the illegal consumption of alcohol and promote responsible drinking. Intervention and prevention efforts should reinforce responsible alcohol consumption. Universities and parents should engage students in the conversation about the collegiate drinking culture and its impact on sexual situations.
- Support services should be in place that help victims cope with the assault, and that are sensitive to victims who report self-blame due to their own intoxication during the sexual assault. In addition, service providers should be aware that victims tend to use alcohol and other substances to cope with this trauma.
- Education efforts concerning sexual assault should address alcohol use. The majority of victims, perpetrators, and bystanders will be under the influence of alcohol or other drugs during sexual assaults and potential sexual assault experiences. Universities and parents should engage students in conversations about how alcohol impacts bodily systems, including memory formation. Additional dialogue should discuss alcohol-related blackouts (i.e., alcohol-induced amnesia) and sexual experiences. Universities should consider clear, comprehensive policies regarding alcohol's role in consent.

3. Reducing barriers to reporting.

Victims of campus sexual assault report significant obstacles when reporting their experiences. These obstacles include individual factors such as fear that others will not believe them or that they will be stigmatized. University related factors include a lack of confidence in the university response and the lack of resources throughout the process. Recommendations for addressing this include:

- Educate all first responders, including staff, faculty, medical staff, victim-services, law enforcement, and bystanders on the importance of their responses.
- Create an effective university process that enables students to feel supported, safe, and protected from additional re-victimization. This process must make sure that students are referred to the correct office and individual.

- Train and educate students on the increased risk and stigmatization for victims of same-sex campus sexual assault.
- As discussed previously, campus culture can create an environment of neglect and indifference with regard to sexual assault and victimization. To counteract this, universities must instead create a culture of awareness about sexual harassment and sexual assault, implement strong support systems for victims, and proactively intervene for females, males, and LGBTQ students when sexual assault has occurred on or off campus.

4. Engaging the community.

Addressing the problem of campus sexual assaults should be recognized as among the fundamental social justice issues currently facing university campuses. The status quo is simply unacceptable. Adequately engaging university communities to counter the sexual assault problem will require combined action involving as many stakeholders as possible.

- Administrators, especially those at the highest ranks, need to take a lead in defining the current situation as unacceptable. Of course, they can provide symbolic support for victims, responders, and those working in prevention of sexual assault, however an effective effort to fix the problem will undoubtedly require a greater allocation of resources, including increased hiring and training of key staff, funding for campus initiatives, and creating an overall supportive environment for those working to address the problem.
- University Disciplinary Boards/Title IX Hearing Panels need increased staffing, training, and financial support from administration, including release from other responsibilities for those who serve in volunteer roles on such panels/boards. In addition, greater review of existing procedures of campus discipline is needed, and best practices should be adopted for investigation, hearing procedures, and sanctioning in cases of sexual assault.
- Faculty, especially in key fields such as sociology, psychology, justice studies, gender studies, and social welfare, should play key roles in highlighting the issue in their instructional and services roles in the university. Creation and facilitation of courses, modules, and campus events/dialogues concerning the sexual assault problem (and possible solutions) is a way that faculty members can raise the issue in their communities, thereby opening up opportunities for dialogue and subsequent action. In addition, faculty members should volunteer

in community service roles addressing the problem, and encourage and nurture student groups and efforts to address the issue.

- Both city police and campus police need explicit training in best practices in encouraging reporting, responding to reports, and investigating sexual assaults, including how to deal with all categories of those reporting: both men and women as victims, LGBTQ victims, and others. Sensitivity to those reporting victimization should be among the best practices, so as to avoid re-victimization.

- The campus community needs to engage various aspects of the problem. These include confronting and changing campus cultures. Key efforts within communities, as nurtured by administration, faculty, and staff, should confront problematic aspects which notably contribute to the problem. These vectors include confronting the party culture of excessive substance use, confronting the persistent rape culture (including rape myths), and confronting hegemonic masculinity in various forms, including the dominance of Greek culture, the valorization of male student athletes, and the lack of acceptance on university campuses of alternative forms of masculinity.

- Parents and students should educate themselves regarding the risks of sexual assault on university campuses, and should demand that universities prioritize this issue. Calls and letters to campus administrators by parents and students often motivate decision-makers to institute programs or allocate resources as a sign that they are taking action on the issue.

Key Resources

Germain, Lauren J. 2016. *Campus Sexual Assault: College Women Respond.* Baltimore, MA: John Hopkins University Press.

Harding, Kate. 2015. *Asking for It: The Alarming Rise of Rape Culture and What We Can Do about It.* Boston, MA: Da Capo Lifelong Books.

Messman-Moore, Terri, Rose Marie Ward, Noga Zerubavel, Rachel B. Chandley, and Sarah N. Barton. 2015. "Emotion Dysregulation and Drinking to Cope as Predictors and Consequences of Alcohol-Involved Sexual Assault: Examination of Short-Term and Long-Term Risk." *Journal of Interpersonal Violence,* 30:601-621. doi: 10.1177/0886260514535259

Murphy, Amy, and Brian Van Brunt. 2016. *Ending Sexual Violence on Campus: A Guide for Practitioners and Faculty.* New York, NY: Routledge.

Paludi, Michele A., ed. 2016. *Campus Action against Sexual Assault: Needs, Policies, Procedures, and Training Programs.* Westport, CT: Praeger.

Sigurvinsdottir, Rannveig, and Sarah E. Ullman. 2015. "Sexual Orientation, Race, and Trauma as Predictors of Sexual Assault Recovery." *Journal of Family Violence, online first*:1-9.

Ward, Rose Marie, Robert N. Bonar, Elizabeth A. Taylor, Kathryn A. Witmer, Craig S. Brinkman, Michael J. Cleveland, and Terri L. Messman-Moore. 2013. "Thursday Drinking and Academic Load Among College Women." *Journal of Studies on Alcohol and Drugs,* 74(6):941-949.

Ward, Rose Marie, Molly R. Matthews, Judith L. Weiner, Kathryn M. Hogan, and Halle C. Popson. 2012. "Alcohol and Sexual Consent Scale: Development and Validation." *American Journal of Health Behavior,* 36(6):746-756.

Wooten, Sara C., and Roland W. Mitchell, eds. 2015. *The Crisis of Campus Sexual Violence: Critical Perspectives on Prevention and Response.* New York, NY: Routledge.

About the Authors

Kristen M. Budd, Ph.D. is an Assistant Professor of Sociology and Social Justice Studies at Miami University. Her research focuses on the intersections between sexual violence, law, and policy. Specifically, she researches various aspects surrounding sexual assault and sexual offenders, such as policies that address sexual assault, public perceptions surrounding sexual offenses and law, and sexual offending behavior itself.

Alana Van Gundy, Ph.D. is an Associate Professor of Justice and Community Studies at Miami University, where she is also the Coordinator of the Criminal Justice Program. In addition to research on sexual assault, she works with incarcerated women. Her research focuses on testing gender-based delinquency models on females to identify gender-specific risk predictor variables, programming efforts, and the intersectionality between race and gender.

Glenn W. Muschert, Ph.D. is a Professor of Sociology and Social Justice Studies at Miami University, and Faculty Affiliate in Comparative Media Studies. His research focuses on mass media dynamics of crime and other social problems, surveillance studies, and the sociology of the Internet.

Rose Marie Ward, Ph.D. is a Professor of Kinesiology and Health at Miami University. In addition, Dr. Ward serves as the Director for the Center for Teaching Excellence. Her research focuses on addictive or harmful behaviors in college students. Specifically, she researches the overlap of alcohol use and sexual assault.

TWO

Missing Rights and Misplaced Justice for Sex Workers in the United States

Crystal A. Jackson and Jennifer J. Reed

The Problem

What does justice look like when talking about prostitution? In the United States, prostitution is highly criminalized under a range of laws, not just one law. Both the sale of sex and the purchase of sex are illegal, as is the solicitation of prostitution (before sex ever takes place). Furthermore, laws such as loitering for the purposes of committing prostitution are based on arbitrary factors that can include a person's location, dress, and possession of more than two condoms. People of color, trans-women, and women living in poverty are often the targets of these laws.

Additionally, since the institutionalization of the Trafficking Victims Protection Act (TVPA) in the early 2000s, the U.S. federal government, with the help of immigration opponents, conservative Christians, and radical (sex worker exclusionary) feminists, has laid the framework for states and municipalities to create new anti-trafficking laws. These laws often revolve around sex trafficking, rather than other forms of labor trafficking. As such, people often assume that prostitution and human trafficking are the same thing – a universal experience of some level of coercion, violence, and/or involving minors – and call to abolish both. In reality, prostitution is paid consensual sex acts between adults. Sex work including prostitution is a complex issue impacted by intersecting inequalities of race, class, and gender.

When so much misinformation guides our students, our policy makers, and our communities, it is essential that the violence and civil rights offenses experienced by those who engage in sex work and the sex trade in the United States be brought to light. Sex work is enmeshed in our understandings of gender and sexual rights, from state-level End Demand campaigns that aim to criminalize those who purchase sex, to high school youth putting on anti-trafficking plays, to recent revelations that Margaret Cho, Laverne Cox, and Maya Angelou, to name a few famous people, have engaged in sex work in the past.

Is the scope and scale of prostitution best understood through the lens of criminal justice? How do we make sense of high levels of police violence and harassment against sex workers (e.g., see Bass 2015), especially trans-women and poor women of color? How does law enforcement determine who should be arrested for prostitution and who should be saved as a victim of sex trafficking? Is rescuing through police raids and arrest—sometimes leading to jail time or mandatory alternatives to incarceration such as yoga or faith-based counseling—the best course of action? What rights are sex workers missing? What does justice for sex workers look like, and who gets to decide that?

Research Evidence

Sex work or the sex trade—engaging in the provision of sexual services in exchange for money, a place to sleep, or other material goods like drugs, food, or clothing—is mired in debates that obfuscate the realities of labor, class inequalities, racial discrimination, migration, and gender norms. In the U.S., this means that rights for sex workers lay at a complex intersection of social problems. Struggles for gender equality, labor rights, and racial equality are also struggles against criminalization and stigma, and sex workers are one group at the center of these struggles.

Yet it is difficult for activists and scholars alike to situate the sale of sex in larger social forces. Blaming "the patriarchy" for prostitution is an overly simplified framework that ignores other social forces like capitalism and gentrification. Instead, research with an intersectional framework finds that some women's choices to enter the industry, and the conditions in which they work, are structured by hierarchies of race, class, and gender. Despite mounting research evidence to the contrary, the conflation of sex work and sex trafficking (i.e., forced or deceptive working conditions) has gone mainstream. Many scholars argue that this conflation of trafficking and work reflects anti-immigrant ideology, and is often rooted in racist, sexist, and transphobic efforts to protect the present power structure.

Further, scholars have shown time and again that prostitution policies hurt those who are arrested, that our public imagination of sex workers as women and girls means that men, male youth, and transgender people are left out of conversations, and that transgender women of color are disproportionately targeted by police for arrest whether they are actually engaging in sex work or not. Much of this data comes from sex worker organizations conducting their own community research projects. We know that male youth are also engaging in the sex trade, we know that the public imagination of pimping and trafficking rarely aligns with the lived realities of hustling on the street alone or with a peer group, yet our laws and our public outcry is all about saving people from the perils of prostitution without actually providing the funding and non-judgmental, voluntary services to help youth of color (under the age of 18) find emancipation, employment, and education or help single mothers find economic stability and housing security.

Recommendations and Solutions

There are several ways in which policy makers, community members, and other key power-holders can redress the missing justice for sex workers:

1. Include sex workers and sex worker rights organizations in policy decisions about prostitution and sex trafficking.

Sex workers' ability to navigate their own labor and safety is rarely given credence by law enforcement, health care agencies, and anti-trafficking advocates. Yet organizations by-and-for-sex-workers have worked for years to provide outreach to sex workers, engage in public education, and advocate for political change, such as:

- Sex Workers Outreach Project (SWOP-USA and local chapters)
- Desiree Alliance, which hosts a national conference for sex workers and allies
- Helping Individual Prostitutes Survive (HIPS) in Washington, D.C.
- Red Umbrella Project in New York City
- St. James Infirmary in San Francisco

This is in addition to numerous organizations that offer outreach and assistance to people who have engaged in the sex trade for survival, like Women with a Vision in New Orleans which addresses HIV/AIDS in communities of color with a focus on African American women, and Streetwise and Safe in New York City which assist homeless LGBTQ youth of color. The voices of sex workers themselves are central to understanding how efforts to protect women—such as new and more punitive sex trafficking laws and prostitution laws—are a form of misplaced justice. Not including sex workers in these conversations and decisions maintains unfair and harmful policies and practices. It also reflects stereotypes that sex workers have little agency to make decisions about their own lives, or are not smart enough to be included in these conversations.

2. *Provide immediate and clear interventions to stop law enforcement harassment and violence against sex workers.*

Sex workers and people in the sex trade have identified police as a main source of violence and harassment: law enforcement officers rape sex workers, physically assault sex workers, coerce sex workers into exchanging sex for not arresting them, and rob sex workers of their money. Law enforcement can legally, in the course of a sting, exchange money for sex, and have sex with the sex worker; after sex, they arrest the worker and take the money back. Police departments are allowed to confiscate the earnings of a sex worker (what is known as civil forfeiture).

Training law enforcement on general competency (e.g., letting women get dressed before arresting them, enforcing consequences for violating sex workers' rights, following through with prosecution of violence) is one way to provide some immediate relief.

3. *Lobby for changes within the criminal justice system.*

Beyond that, lobbying for changes within the criminal justice system at large can take many shapes. For example, police departments can be pressured to stop doing prostitution stings in person and online. A vast majority of sex work takes place indoors, but studies and media attention have focused on street-based prostitution, which paints a skewed perspective to policy makers, social advocates, and the general public. Police therefore tend to target marginalized populations for arrest: street-based sex workers who are often poor women of color, or transwomen of color assumed to be sex workers. However, police and FBI can, and should be pressured to end anti-trafficking "rescue" operations where arresting the victims of trafficking is normal procedure.

In addition, Offices of District Attorneys can make the decision to not pressure online services like Craigslist to remove or end adult content. In the 21st century, the forms of policing are changing to catch up to technologically savvy sex workers. Recent raids on websites—like Rentboy.com—and demands that other websites refuse to host sexual service advertisements—like Craigslist.com—have been met with outcry from sex workers themselves. Removing their means of screening clients pushes prostitution further underground and makes it more dangerous to work, not less.

Further, judges and courts can make the choice to not hear or not sentence prostitution cases. Some jurisdictions have moved to parallel the drug courts' approaches to alternative sentencing—counseling or non-profit intervention instead of jail time. However, there are many critiques of mandatory counseling alternatives, and sex workers (and some scholars) argue that alternative sentencing strengthens the growing use of non-profits as a form of policing, another arm of the criminal justice system.

4. Address the root causes of poverty.

Poverty has deep implications for racial justice and transgender justice. The slogan "Outlaw Poverty Not Prostitution" has been a rallying cry for U.S. sex worker activists since the 1970s, and it still holds truth today. While many sex workers report finding that the work suits their financial needs, a common concern is that others may be more limited by poverty or other vulnerable living situations that create economic compulsion. To address this legitimate concern we must deal with the broader underlying root causes, and support policies and programs that make available affordable long-term housing, living wage jobs, and accessible education opportunities.

5. Create and support large-scale legal change to the criminal justice system: decriminalize prostitution.

Overall, the best way to ensure all of the above is decriminalization. To address the inequities around sex work, many advocates and scholars argue that decriminalization offers the strongest starting point for providing assistance (as do the World Health Organization, the United Nations, and Human Rights Watch, all of whom have come out in favor of decriminalization). In 2015, the global human rights organization Amnesty International voted to adopt a policy that supports the full decriminalization of all aspects of consensual sex work. In this same year, to address health concerns, the editors of a 2015 special issue of the British medical journal *The Lancet* called on governments to decriminalize sex work as the most effective measure to prevent the spread of HIV.

There is a lot of confusion around what "decriminalization" means as applied to prostitution. The term simply refers to the removal of criminal penalties against consensual adults trading sex acts for explicit compensation. Decriminalization also denotes that both workers and consumers have access to the same legal protection afforded to all other citizens. In New Zealand, after three years of parliamentary debate, the Prostitution Reform Act 2003 was passed. It took the laws out of the criminal code and placed them under the business code. Known as one of the most liberal policies in the world, it decriminalized brothels, escort agencies, and soliciting prostitution. Studies since then have shown that decriminalization has led to safer sex practices and the ability to report crimes without fear of arrest. The law still prohibits prostitution for anyone under 18 years of age, which means that youth who are engaging in the sex trade find it difficult to secure social services.

There are attempts to create legal change in the United States. The Erotic Service Providers Legal, Education, and Research Project (ESPLERP) filed a federal lawsuit on March 4, 2015 to challenge the criminalization of prostitution in California. The lawsuit argues that banning prostitution is unconstitutional because it violates the First Amendment by hindering the right of U.S. sex workers to engage in consensual, private activities. San Francisco and Berkeley entertained prostitution decriminalization efforts within city limits (Proposition K, San Francisco in 2008; Measure Q, Berkeley in 2004). Although these efforts failed, they did garner a fair percentage of votes (see www. bayswan.org/SFInitiative08/ for more information). Just this year, three female legislators in New Hampshire put forth a bipartisan state bill to decriminalize prostitution.

Yet decriminalization is a rare political approach globally, and seemingly an unviable option in the U.S. right now. Instead, many Western countries have some form of a legalization model. In the U.S., the only current legal model for prostitution is in the state of Nevada. Women in Nevada are only permitted to work in licensed brothels in particular rural counties. Even this is suspect as many legalization models are reliant on heteronormative stereotypes of sex purchasers as men, and workers as women who are considered potential vectors of disease, requiring overly zealous health screenings and registration requirements.

Likewise, criminalizing the buyer of sex makes sex workers less safe. Some policy makers and activists (feminist and non-feminist alike) argue that women who sell sex should not be criminalized, but their clients should—an approach popularized as "end demand" or "the Swedish model." In 1999, Sweden put this into law and this approach is touted by neo-abolitionists—activists who draw parallels between slavery and sex trafficking—as a response to prostitution and violence. Nonetheless, sex worker rights organizations and academics find that this approach to reduce or end "demand" is a miscalculation of the actual inequalities that sex workers face.

6. Finally, legal change does not automatically lead to social change. Social stigma, poverty, sexism, transphobia, racism, and other forms of oppression must be addressed through public education and policies alike.

Decriminalization could be a first step toward establishing basic rights for people who engage in the sex trade and those profiled as prostitutes, but criminalization is just one problem. In the U.S., would decriminalization provide relief to sex workers or might it also open doors to increasingly harsh anti-trafficking efforts? We must take seriously efforts to protect all workers and enforce labor standards, including for migrants, documented or undocumented. Poverty, social class inequalities, discrimination and exploitation of undocumented immigrants, and law enforcement profiling and use of social services to monitor and punish marginalized individuals must also be addressed to account for the misplaced justice for sex workers.

Key Resources

Web Resources

Amnesty International. 2015. "Global Movement Votes to Adopt Policy to Protect Human Rights of Sex Workers." https://www.amnesty.org/en/latest/news/2015/08/global-movement-votes-to-adopt-policy-to-protect-human-rights-of-sex-workers/

Bay Area Sex Worker Advocacy Network (BAYSWAN). Produces the San Francisco Bay Area Sex Worker Film and Arts Festival, and provides consultation about sex worker rights issues. http://www.bayswan. org/contact.html

Desiree Alliance. A sex worker–led network working in harm reduction, political advocacy, and health services for sex workers. http:// desireealliance.org/wordpress/

Global Network of Sex Work Projects (NSWP). Facilitates development of networks of sex workers and sex work advocacy projects. http:// www.nswp.org

Red Umbrella Project. 2014. "Criminal, Victim, or Worker?: NYC Human Trafficking Intervention Courts' Impact on People in the Sex Trade." http://redumbrellaproject.org/advocate/nyhtic/

Sex Workers Outreach Project (SWOP-USA). A social justice network to protect the human rights of people involved in the sex trade and their communities. http://www.swopusa.org

Sex Workers Project (SWP). Provides legal and social services to sex workers, regardless of their situation. https://swp.urbanjustice.org

Young Women's Empowerment Project. 2012. "Denied Help!: How Youth in the Sex Trade and Street Economy are Turned Away from Systems Meant to Help Us & What We are Doing to Fight Back." https:// ywepchicago.files.wordpress.com/2012/09/bad-encounter-line-report-2012.pdf

Print Resources

Agustín, Laura. 2007. *Sex at the Margins: Migration, Labour Markets and the Rescue Industry*. London, UK: Zed Books.

Bass, Alison. 2015. *Getting Screwed: Sex Workers and the Law*. Lebanon, NH: University Press of New England.

Bernstein, Elizabeth. 2012. "Carceral Politics as Gender Justice? The 'Traffic in Women' and Neoliberal Circuits of Crime, Sex, and Rights." *Theory and Society*. 41(3):233-259.

Brents, Barbara G., Crystal A. Jackson, and Kathryn Hausbeck. 2010. *The State of Sex: Tourism, Sex, and Sin in the New American Heartland*. New York, NY: Routledge.

Chateauvert, Melinda. 2014. *Sex Workers Unite: A History of the Movement from Stonewall to Slutwalk*. Boston, MA: Beacon Press.

Human Rights Violations of Sex Workers, People in the Sex Trades, and People Profiled as Such. 2014. *Submission to the United Nations Universal Periodic Review of the United States of America.* Submitted September 2014 for the Second Cycle of the 22nd Session of the Working Group on the Universal Periodic Review Human Rights Council (May 2015).

Kempadoo, Kamala, Jyoti Sanghera, and Bandana Pattanaik, eds. 2011. *Trafficking and Prostitution Reconsidered: New Perspectives on Migration, Sex Work, and Human Rights* (2nd Edition). New York, NY: Routledge.

Weitzer, Ronald. 2012. *Legalizing Prostitution: From Illicit Vice to Lawful Business.* New York, NY: New York University Press.

About the Authors

Crystal A. Jackson, Ph.D. is an assistant professor of Sociology, and affiliated Gender Studies faculty, at the John Jay College-City University of New York. She is a long-time sex worker rights activist. Crystal is co-author of *The State of Sex: Tourism, Sex, and Sin in the New American Heartland* (Routledge, 2010).

Jennifer J. Reed, M.A. is a Ph.D. candidate in Sociology at the University of Nevada, Las Vegas. She, along with another graduate student, accepted the 2011 SSSP Social Action Award on behalf of Sex Workers Outreach Project Las Vegas. She then served as the chapter's co-director in 2014. Jennifer conducted outreach and interviews with youth involved in the sex trades in Las Vegas as part of a national multi-city study supported by the U.S. Department of Justice. She testified at the 2013 Nevada legislature for evidence-based sex trafficking policy for which she now has an invited piece published in *Sociologists in Action on Inequalities: Race, Class, Gender, and Sexuality*. Jennifer is a proud mom, grandma, and avid social justice activist.

SECTION II

Public and Environmental Health

THREE

Factory Farming: Impacts and Potential Solutions

Ryan Gunderson, Diana Stuart, and Brian Petersen

The Problem

The majority of animal-derived products in the U.S. today come from "factory farms." Due to the agricultural revolution of the mid-twentieth century, farm animals have been increasingly relocated from open pastures to large feedlots and warehouses called "concentrated animal feeding operations" (CAFOs). Animal agriculture today is a capital-intensive and mechanized process whereby ownership and control has shifted from families to a relatively small number of large agribusiness corporations. The United States Department of Agriculture (USDA) shows that this trend toward larger farms, driven by the motive to increase profits through new technologies and large volume production, has intensified since the late 1980s in all industries, with the greatest increases in the dairy and hog industries. The typical animal product comes from larger and larger operations, leading to fewer small farms, which are unable to compete with the resources of large factory farms. Many family farmers today do not directly own the majority of their operation, as they have become merely subcontractors for large agribusinesses. According to the Food and Agricultural Organization of the United Nations (FAO), this trend toward larger operations is projected to continue worldwide.

The rise and proliferation of factory farming has raised a number of social, economic, and ethical concerns. A wealth of research from environmental and animal scientists, public health scholars, sociologists, as well as governmental and non-governmental organizations has revealed the massive scale of factory farming's negative impacts on public health, the environment, and animal welfare. In what follows, we concisely summarize the research on these three problem areas and then provide informed recommendations for public policy solutions and social action. We offer specific policy recommendations to address some of the worst impacts of industrial animal agriculture in the short-term, but also argue that long-term strategies to transition to plant-based diets and to diversify the goals of food production (beyond profitability) are needed to address the interrelated root causes of public health, environmental, and animal welfare problems.

The Research

Public Health Impacts

Various bacterial and viral pathogens are linked to CAFOs and slaughterhouses due to contamination from animal manure. Usually originating from cattle manure, people ingest *Escherichia coli* O157:H7 through water or food, which can cause bloody diarrhea, seizures, comas, severe kidney damage, and death. *Salmonella* and *Campylobacter* are bacteria associated with chickens and can contaminate food through feces, leading to stomach pains, diarrhea, and, less commonly, death. The introduction and spread of pathogens in food is exacerbated by cost-cutting practices such as increasing line speeds in slaughterhouses and processing plants. In addition, companies process large volumes of food in centralized facilities where cross-contamination can impact thousands of individuals as the products are distributed across vast geographic areas.

Bovine spongiform encephalopathy (BSE) ("mad cow disease" and Creutzfeldt-Jakob disease in human form) and H1N1 ("swine flu") have infected thousands. The USDA believes that BSE developed and was expanded by feeding calves the meat and bone meal of other cattle, which is a factory farming technique to cut costs. Gregory Gray, the director of the Center for Emerging Infectious Diseases at the University of Iowa College of Public Health, speculates that the H1N1 outbreak too was likely caused through factory farming practices, but there is no conclusive evidence showing where the strain developed. The Pew Environment Group and similar organizations say the lack of data is because most university research of animal agriculture is funded by industry sources with a financial conflict of interest. Along with bacterial and viral pathogens, tissue growth-related materials such as heavy metals, phosphorus, hormones, and pharmaceuticals have all been found in factory farming tainted drinking and recreational water.

In 2011, the Food and Drug Administration estimated that around 80 percent of all antibiotics manufactured in the U.S. are fed to farm animals. The large majority of these are used for "nontherapeutic" purposes, which means to promote rapid tissue growth. Scientists, many governments, and the United Nations are increasingly concerned about more quickly developing and more diverse antibiotic-resistant strains of bacteria (many of the antibiotics fed to farm animals are related to antibiotics used by humans). Although more research is needed to project long-term impacts, the massive amount of veterinary pharmaceuticals fed to animals in CAFOs is one of the leading public health concerns related to factory farming.

Factory farming is often seen as an environmental justice issue because groups already at risk disproportionately bear the environmental health harms of factory farming: rural communities, farm and slaughterhouse workers, and the global poor. Researchers at the University of Iowa's Environmental Health Sciences Research Center found that rural communities rarely want CAFOs nearby, so they are disproportionately placed in low-income areas with less political influence. Rural communities are shown to be at greater risks for a number of physical, mental, and social health problems due to neighboring CAFOs, including respiratory problems, anxiety, post-traumatic stress disorder, and depression. Relatedly, numerous studies show that CAFO and slaughterhouse workers labor in relatively unsafe and unsanitary work environments. Sociologist Philip McMichael argued that as meat consumption increases worldwide, food is reallocated from the poor to the rich because the global poor still depend on grains for sustenance, which are redirected to feed animals for the meat industries. This is related to a paradox in the health impacts of contemporary animal production and consumption, as argued by researchers from the Johns Hopkins School of Public Health: around one billion people are overweight or obese largely due to increased meat consumption (as animal products are the primary source of saturated fats) while around one billion people are malnourished in part due to reduced crop availability.

Environmental Impacts and Climate Change

The FAO reports that processes associated with livestock production account for 70 percent of all agricultural land use, occupying 30 percent of the Earth's surface and contributing to land degradation and biodiversity loss. Animal agriculture uses a significant amount of fresh water. Estimates of how much water is required to produce 1 kilogram of beef vary widely, due to the production system and feed used, as well as how much of the production chain is included. Beef production requires much more water than other livestock, and far more than crops. Mekonnen and Hoekstra's 2012 study of global water consumption calculates that producing 1 ton of beef requires 15,400 cubic meters of water, 20 times per calorie more than needed for cereals and starchy roots. These inputs contribute to significant water withdrawals and pollution, as well as increasing land, water, and soil degradation associated with intensive cropland production.

One dairy cow produces as much waste as 20 to 40 humans, contributing to drinking water contamination and water and air pollution. Much of the synthetic nitrogen produced to grow feed for farm animals is inefficiently absorbed by crops and animals. This unabsorbed nitrogen ends up in water and the air through pathways such as manure runoff, manure lagoon overflows, and leaching. Nitrogen leached into water comes from not only animal manure but also from corn and soybean production, much of which goes to feed livestock. Nitrogen oxides in the air increase the risk of asthma, reactive airways disease, chronic respiratory disease, and respiratory tract inflammation, among other health problems. Nitrate in groundwater is commonly linked to reproductive problems, "blue-baby" syndrome, and various cancers. In addition, more pesticides are needed for increased feed production, increasing harm to biodiversity and human health risks including cancer, poisoning, and immune, reproductive, and nervous system damage.

Dairy production has a direct consequence for water quality by contributing to fecal coliform pollution in waterways. In 1995, the Washington State Department of Ecology identified fecal coliform and decreased oxygen levels as primary water quality problems in the state, largely due to dairies. This pollution led to direct consequences for salmon spawning and rearing, an important and endangered species in the region. This example highlights both the direct consequences meat production has on water quality but also showcases how industrial animal production causes environmental problems in the commons more broadly.

According to the FAO, animal agriculture is estimated to emit 14.5 percent of total anthropogenic greenhouse gases. The EPA reports that microbial fermentation from livestock contributes over 23 percent of all US methane emissions and manure management contributes an additional 8 percent. In addition, nitrous oxide gas, mentioned above, is also a powerful greenhouse gas, with approximately 300 times the heating capacity of carbon dioxide. Overall, the FAO reports that livestock production currently produces 7.1 gigatons of carbon dioxide equivalents per year: over 14 percent of total anthropogenic greenhouse gas emissions. Cattle production alone accounts for 65 percent of this total.

Animal Welfare Issues

CAFO-housed animals are usually confined and fattened as fast as possible with unnatural diets and growth-promoters, processes that are painful for animals. Some of the welfare issues associated with factory farming include: the forced molting of hens; broiler chicken lameness; the constricted confinement of pregnant and lactating sows in individual crates; digestive and digestive-related disorders among beef cattle; painful bacterial infections of the udder tissues (mastitis) among dairy cows; and veal calves spending the entirety of their lives in small crates. In short, factory-farmed animals live painful and relatively short lives and are unable to express most natural behaviors. Animal ethicists have put forth normative reasons from a variety of perspectives—which cannot be reviewed here—about why humans should care about farm animal suffering. But even if one is unconcerned with animal suffering, the same forces and processes that harm animals also harm the environment and public health. For example, concentrating animals into large feedlots is painful for animals due to limited mobility and is harmful for public health and the environment due to the concentration of manure.

Recommendations and Solutions

Current governmental policies from the local to federal levels fail to adequately mitigate and prevent factory farming's negative impacts on the health of humans, the environment, and farm animals. In this section, we discuss some possible actions to address these issues and offer recommendations in two forms. The first consists of incremental policy recommendations that are politically feasible at this time. The purpose is to lessen some of the most egregious harms of factory farming in the short-term. The second is an outline for system-wide changes that, although less politically and socially feasible at this time, would be necessary for a viable, long-term solution: (1) transitioning away from the consumption of animal products as well as (2) confronting the underlying driver of human, animal, and environmental degradation, a system that prioritizes profitability before well-being.

1. Short-term policy reforms.

Public Health

Antibiotic resistance poses one of the most serious human health risks related to animal agriculture. Policies that require veterinarian prescriptions for all applications of antibiotics to farm animals would reduce widespread over-application. To protect consumers from foodborne illness, cost-cutting practices that result in the introduction and spread of contaminants need to be restricted. These practices include the use of fast line speeds in food processing facilities and processing large volumes of food in centralized processing plants. To address the cost-cutting practices that led to "mad cow disease," the use of all mammalian protein in the feed of livestock that will enter the human food supply should be banned, as recommended by the Center for Food Safety. Education programs aimed at reducing the consumption of meat and dairy could reduce the prevalence of specific diseases associated with consuming animal products. The federal government and the agencies responsible for animal husbandry, food safety, and public health would be the most appropriate to implement these reforms (the USDA and FDA). However, funding for these agencies to conduct inspections and enforce current regulations has been reduced. New regulations are needed that ban the use of cost-cutting strategies when they adversely affect public health along with adequate funding for monitoring and enforcement.

Environment

Many alternative practices have been developed that can increase efficient water use, improve waste management, and reduce pollution and greenhouse gas emissions from livestock operations. However, the adoption of these practices remains largely voluntary. While certain practices may be suitable for adoption in all CAFO operations and could be required by new federal laws, allowing farm managers to choose which practices work best in their operation is more politically feasible. Some environmental groups support market-based cap and trade programs to address pollution; however, these can be ineffective or detrimental if not implemented carefully. Taxing greenhouse gas emissions and other pollutants is likely to be more effective. Taxes could be calculated, monitored, and enforced by either a regulatory agency or a third-party contracted by the federal government. A tiered tax on the number of livestock could also be an effective policy to reduce the size of CAFOs. In addition, federal policies aimed at minimizing new CAFOs or land conversion to cropland for growing animal feed could reduce deforestation and the endangerment of wildlife.

Animal Welfare

A first step to improve animal welfare would be to ban especially cruel and mutilating practices, like the debeaking of egg-laying hens, and to require animal breeders to specifically select for traits that reduce suffering. In addition, new laws should increase cage size and ban the use of battery cages for hens, crates for veal calves, and other inhumane conditions. California banned the use of battery cages, gestation crates for sows, and restrictive veal stalls with the passage of the Prevention of Farm Animal Cruelty Act in 2008. However, in general, farm animal welfare legislation in the U.S. is still very weak. For example, the core law protecting U.S. farm animals, the Humane Slaughter Act, excludes chickens from its protection, which account for about 95 percent of all farm animals. In comparison, the EU Strategy for the Protection and Welfare of Animals calls for farm animals to be free from discomfort; hunger and thirst; fear and distress; pain, injury and disease; as well as having the freedom to express natural behaviors. We support this program. The strongest initial step toward accomplishing these goals is to implement the Prevention of Farm Animal Cruelty Act at a federal level.

2. Long-term strategies for systemic change.

A Shift to Plant-based Diets

Many of the problems described above can be lessened with policies that will reduce the number of animals in agriculture. Replacing animal products with alternatives based on soy, wheat, and other high protein plant "analogs" would reduce the total number of animals in agriculture and address a number of issues. A Worldwatch Institute analysis predicts that a 25 percent reduction in animal products worldwide by 2017 would yield at least a 12.5 percent reduction in greenhouse gas emissions. This would also reduce the amount of water and land used by animal agriculture and the amount of waste and pollution it produces. Eating fewer animal products would also reduce chances of foodborne illness and other detrimental health effects. The United Nations Environment Programme's International Panel for Sustainable Resource Management calls for a worldwide shift away from consumption of animals due to its unsustainable impacts upon the environment. An increase in plant-based diets could feed more people worldwide, with fewer agricultural inputs, saving costly resources and improving human and environmental health, as well as leading to less suffering for farm animals.

The Worldwatch Institute argues that increased marketing will increase sales for meat and dairy analogs and reduce the need for consumption of animal products. Governments levying a tax per animal, on animal products, or on the estimated emissions of greenhouse gases and pollution would encourage smaller animal agriculture operations and increased investment in protein alternatives. Corporations would likely add the new tax expense to the price of the product, resulting in less consumption of animal products. In addition, campaigns to expose the realities of CAFOs could be used to educate the public. Using taxes, marketing, and educational programs, dietary changes could happen quickly.

Currently most advocacy groups remain focused on a specific issue related to either human health, animal welfare, or the environment. However, unless we see these issues as interrelated, our solutions will result in only marginal improvements. We agree that a worldwide movement toward plant-based diets is the long-term solution. Achieving this goal will require a change in values and priorities, and a transition to a society that places human and animal well-being and the environment above corporate profits.

Diversifying and Reprioritizing Social Goals

The policies, reforms, and interventions described in the short-term policy section above can reduce some negative impacts of factory farming but will not result in the systemic change that is necessary to fully address these persistent problems. The current policy approach, focused on market-based reforms and consumer choice, is not sufficient in light of the current and projected increases in the production and consumption of factory farmed products worldwide. A viable and enduring solution entails opposition to the underlying drivers, namely growth-dependency and profit-maximization. A society that adopts sustainable plant-based diets may sit outside the barriers of a socioeconomic system that necessitates profit-maximization at the expense of public health, environmental health, and animal welfare. At a minimum, it would require a socioeconomic system that diversifies the goals of food production beyond profit-maximization.

We do not prescribe policy recommendations to reach this goal because it first requires a successful anti-systemic social movement. This movement would transform dominant ideologies and values to support governance that protects people, animals, and the environment above other considerations. Current economic priorities continue to lead to degradation and suffering experienced widely. Therefore, in order to best work toward systemic change, social movements against factory farming should first connect with other movements with overlapping concerns, such as the labor and degrowth movements.

Key Resources

Center for Food Safety (CFS) http://www.centerforfoodsafety.org CFS is a national non-profit public interest and environmental advocacy organization working to protect human health and the environment by curbing the use of harmful food production technologies and promoting organic and other forms of sustainable agriculture.

Donham, Kelley J., Steven Wing, David Osterberg, Jan L. Flora, Carol Hodne, Kendall M. Thu, and Peter S. Thorne. 2007. "Community Health and Socioeconomic Issues Surrounding Concentrated Animal Feeding Operations." *Environmental Health Perspectives* 115(2):317-320. Retrieved March 21, 2016. http://ir.uiowa.edu/cgi/viewcontent.cgi?article=1022&context=oeh_pubs

Food and Agricultural Organization of the United Nations. 2013. *Tackling Climate Change through Livestock: A Global Assessment of Emissions and Mitigation Opportunities.* Rome: FAO; 2006. Retrieved March 21, 2016. http://www.fao.org/docrep/018/i3437e/i3437e.pdf

Goodland, Robert and Jeff Anhang. 2009. "Livestock and Climate Change: What if the Key Actors in Climate Change were Pigs, Chickens and Cows?" *World Watch*, November/December, pp. 10-19. Retrieved March 21, 2016. http://www.worldwatch.org/files/pdf/Livestock%20and%20Climate%20Change.pdf

MacDonald, James M. and William D. McBride. 2009. "The Transformation of U.S. Livestock Agriculture: Scale, Efficiency, and Risks." Economic Research Service. EIB-43. United States Department of Agriculture. Retrieved March 21, 2016. http://www.ers.usda.gov/publications/eib-economic-information-bulletin/eib43.aspx

McMichael, Philip. 2008. *Development and Social Change: A Global Perspective*. Los Angeles, CA: Pine Forge Press.

Schmidt, Charles W. 2009. "Swine CAFOs & Novel H1N1 Flu: Separating Facts from Fears." *Environmental Health Perspectives* 117(9): A394-A401. Retrieved March 21, 2016. http://ehp.niehs.nih.gov/117-a394/

United Nations Environment Programme. 2010. *Assessing the Environmental Impacts of Production and Consumption: Priority Products and Materials*. International Panel for Sustainable Resource Management. Retrieved March 21, 2016. http://www.unep.org/resourcepanel/Portals/24102/PDFs/PriorityProductsAndMaterials_Summary_EN.pdf

United States Environmental Protection Agency. N.d. "What's the Problem?" Retrieved March 21, 2016. http://www3.epa.gov/region9/animalwaste/problem.html

United States Environmental Protection Agency. 2016. "Draft U.S. Greenhouse Gas Inventory Report: 1990-2014. Chapter 5: Agriculture." Retrieved March 21, 2016. http://www3.epa.gov/climatechange/Downloads/ghgemissions/US-GHG-Inventory-2016-Chapter-5-Agriculture.pdf

About the Authors

Ryan Gunderson, Ph.D. is an Assistant Professor of Sociology and Social Justice Studies in the Department of Sociology and Gerontology at Miami University. He has published multiple articles on environmental, public health, and animal welfare concerns of industrial animal agriculture. By adopting environmental sociological perspectives, Ryan's analyses emphasize political-economic drivers in the creation and maintenance of factory farming and the unequal distribution of its negative consequences. His current research projects in this area include, with colleagues, a conceptual piece on the commodification of farm animals and a public health policy study on demographic and social psychological predictors for support for plant-based diets.

Diana Stuart, Ph.D. is an Assistant Professor in the Sustainable Communities Program and in the School of Earth Sciences and Environmental Sustainability at Northern Arizona University. Her research examines environmental and social issues in industrial agriculture and how to transition to a more sustainable food system. She has researched leafy greens production, strawberries, corn, soy, and dairy. Her work has explored ways to increase wild biodiversity, reduce fertilizer pollution and greenhouse gas emissions, and support animal welfare.

Brian Petersen, Ph.D. is an Assistant Professor in the Department of Geography, Planning and Recreation at Northern Arizona University. His research and published work focuses on climate change adaptation and landscape level conservation. His work draws on both social and natural science perspectives to interrogate contemporary natural resource and environmental challenges. Currently, his research focus centers on the climate change adaptation actions and plans put forth by the National Park Service and the US Forest Service in the Western United States.

FOUR

Solutions to the Social Problem of Food Insecurity in the United States

Leslie Hossfeld, Brooke Kelly, and Julia Waity

The Problem

Food insecurity is a much bigger social problem in the United States than many imagine. When the average person thinks of food insecurity, the first thing that may come to mind is people starving in low-income nations. While that is a social problem that needs to be addressed, it is crucial to understand that food insecurity is also an issue in high-income nations, namely the United States. While there are U.S. programs that provide food assistance to those who are food insecure, there may not be enough food from those sources to last families through the month. Food is one place where households can cut money from their budget. Unlike the rent, which might result in eviction, or the electric bill, which might result in the power being turned off, food expenditures are not a fixed cost. A family may be forced to choose between heat and food if their money is running low. The consequences of food insecurity include poor health outcomes such as increased morbidity and mortality as well as depression. For children, being food insecure can lead to poor performance in school. Food insecurity coexists in the United States with high rates of industrial food waste. The problem of food insecurity is one that we, as a wealthy nation, can no longer ignore. In addition to the pain and suffering food insecurity incurs on individuals, the social costs to public health and potential lost talent are too high.

The Research Evidence

Food insecurity is defined as a lack of access to enough food at all times for all members of the household to be healthy and active. The official measure of food insecurity in the United States is established through the Current Population Survey's Food Security Supplement. Respondents are asked to respond to a variety of questions and statements, from "We worried whether our food would run out before we got money to buy more" to "In the last 12 months did you or other adults in your household ever not eat for a whole day because there wasn't enough money for food?" In 2014, 14.0 percent of Americans were food insecure. While this represents a decrease from the almost 15 percent of Americans who were food insecure during the Great Recession, the US still has not reached pre-recession levels of around 10-11 percent. Also, 5.6 percent of Americans experienced very low food security in 2014, which means food intake was reduced and normal eating patterns were disrupted. Rural and principal city areas tend to have higher rates of food insecurity, as does the southern region of the United States, with the highest food insecurity in Mississippi at 22.0 percent. While not all those who are poor are food insecure, and not all who are food insecure are poor, poverty and food insecurity are closely intertwined, with 39.5 percent of households below the poverty line reporting food insecurity, while only 6.3 percent of households above 185 percent of the poverty line report food insecurity.

While the child poverty rate is higher than the adult poverty rate (21.1 percent for those under 18 versus 13.5 percent for ages 18-64 using U.S. Census Bureau data), the food insecurity rate for households with children is higher than for all households (19.2 percent versus 14 percent using Current Population Survey data), but 9.8 percent of that number is adults only, which means that food insecure adults and children in those households only make up 9.4 percent. This may be due to the fact that parents protect their children from food insecurity by first skipping meals or cutting back for themselves before they allow their children to go hungry. It may also be the case that parents underreport food insecurity in their children because they do not want to seem like bad parents.

Food insecurity is often associated with living in a food desert. The 2008 Farm Bill included language that defined a food desert as an "area in the United States with limited access to affordable and nutritious food, particularly such an area composed of predominantly lower income neighborhoods and communities." Food deserts can lead to higher rates of obesity and other diet-related diseases. While food deserts may not directly cause food insecurity, they are good indicators of areas where food insecurity is more likely—in low-income communities, which are disproportionately, but not exclusively, populated by African Americans, Hispanics, and other marginalized racial and ethnic groups.

Those who are food insecure rely on a variety of resources in order to get enough to eat. The most commonly used are federal nutrition assistance programs, with 61 percent of food insecure households reporting participation in these programs. These encompass a variety of programs including the Supplemental Nutrition Assistance Program (SNAP), Women Infants and Children (WIC), and the National School Lunch Program (free and reduced price lunch and breakfast). SNAP, commonly known as food stamps, provides monetary benefits on a debit-type card that can be used to purchase most grocery items. WIC is similar, but the items are limited and it is only for pregnant and postpartum women and children up to age five. In addition, or instead of those programs, individuals who are food insecure may rely on community-based programs like food pantries and soup kitchens. Food pantries provide a small amount of groceries, usually intended to last several days to a week, while soup kitchens provide prepared meals to eat at the soup kitchen, or sometimes to take away.

Recommendations and Solutions

The authors of this chapter have several recommendations for changes to existing programs and calls for new action that can begin to more effectively redress the significant problem of food insecurity in the United States.

1. *Federal programs.*

- *SNAP.* Work requirements are one example of ineffective policies imposed on SNAP participants. According to the Center on Budget and Policy Priorities, SNAP is a responsive program that is used by more people when there are fewer jobs, and fewer people when there are more jobs. Particularly burdensome are recent decisions by some states to impose SNAP time-limits that cut off recipients' access to benefits, despite a state's ability to implement a waiver when their state has high unemployment or a declining labor market. The report goes on to say that more than 500,000 of our nation's poorest people will be affected and will lose SNAP benefits; many in the South will be hit "particularly hard." The time limit is part of the 1996 welfare law that limits individuals to three months of SNAP benefits in any 36 month period when they are not employed or in a work training program for at least 20 hours a week. Additional barriers to receiving SNAP should not be imposed on this important program that does a great deal to alleviate food insecurity, and poverty as well.

- *Free and Reduced School Lunch and Breakfast.* Steps are already being taken to expand another federal nutrition program, free and reduced price lunch and breakfast for school age children. Some areas have adopted community eligibility, where if 40 percent of students qualify for free meals, all students are made eligible. Universally applied approaches such as this, as opposed to means tested approaches targeting specific populations, break down some of the social stigma barriers that exist for students in utilizing these programs. An awareness campaign should be implemented so that child nutrition directors in schools across the nation increase awareness and participation in these options, as well as in summer feeding programs (described below), which are significantly underutilized.
- *Bridging Programs for Children.* Several programs serve to bridge the gap in need during the summer months and weekends when children do not have access to school breakfast and lunch programs. Awareness campaigns about the availability of these programs are needed and additional funding for these programs is paramount.

  o Backpack programs have emerged to provide children who rely on free and reduced lunch programs with nutritional staple items sent home with them in backpacks over the weekends. These programs are typically run through local food banks that source food from the United States Department of Agriculture (USDA).
  o Summer food service programs are federally funded programs that serve healthy meals to children and teens in low-income areas during the summer months, in neighborhood schools, parks, community centers, and places of worship. Though growing, such programs are significantly underutilized. For children who are in isolated rural areas or experience other transportation barriers in accessing traditional summer feeding sites, mobile feeding models have emerged as a creative solution to increase access.

o Mobile feeding trucks serve not only children during summer months, but children, adults, and the elderly throughout the year as well. This approach seeks to address typical barriers to accessing services, such as lack of transportation and geographical isolation. For services such as SNAP and mobile feeding sites, many of those who are eligible do not receive these benefits. There are many compounding reasons for this: lack of knowledge about the program and their eligibility, inadequate public and private transportation options, lack of child care, language barriers, and social stigma attached to receiving assistance. To address food insecurity effectively, policies and solutions must consider all barriers to participation for those in need and find ways to increase awareness and access to services.

2. Food pantries.

Food pantries and soup kitchens are being over-utilized as the Great Recession continues to impact the food insecure population, making some who were previously food secure now insecure, and worsening the situation for those already suffering from food insecurity. Additional funding could help these agencies in the important work they are doing to supplement or substitute for federal nutrition assistance programs.

College campuses are increasingly responding to food insecurity of those in the communities in which the college is located as well as food insecure students on campus. Campus food pantries have emerged on college campuses throughout the U.S. as the recession and the increasing costs of college leave some students food insecure. Campus kitchen programs have also emerged on college campuses as a means to serve those who experience food insecurity outside of the campus. These student-led programs make use of prepared food from the cafeteria that would otherwise go to waste. This food is repurposed and donated to local soup kitchens.

3. Community food systems.

Supporting community food systems initiatives holds the greatest likelihood of creating substantive, meaningful, long-term change in food insecurity. Since this requires systems-change, all elements of the food system must be examined. The Cornell University report *A Primer on Community Food Systems: Linking Food, Nutrition and Agriculture* describes community food systems as a: "system in which food production, processing, distribution and consumption are integrated to enhance the environmental, economic, social and nutritional health of a particular place" (http://www.farmlandinfo.org/sites/default/files/Primer_1.pdf). The concept of community food systems is sometimes used interchangeably with "local" or "regional" food systems but by including the word "community" there is an emphasis on strengthening existing (or developing new) relationships between all components of the food system. This reflects a prescriptive approach to building a food system, one that holds sustainability—economic, environmental, and social—as a long-term goal toward which a community strives.

The transformative power of implementing this vision of local/community food systems creates positive and sustainable economic development. These system-change efforts are beginning to take shape across the United States. Increased federal funding to support these initiatives is imperative in building food secure, inclusive, healthy communities. Recommendations that will facilitate expansion of these initiatives include:

- *USDA funding streams*—Increase funding streams for community food projects through National Institute of Food and Agriculture (NIFA) and Agriculture and Food Research Initiative (AFRI) funding programs.
- *Expand FoodCorps*—FoodCorps is an AmeriCorps Volunteers in Service to America (VISTA) federal program that places service volunteers in partner schools across the nation to work with children and communities to learn how to grow healthy food and create healthy children.
- *Create Local Food Extension Agents in every county through NIFA*—NIFA is an agency within the USDA that funds local and state research, education and extension programs related to agriculture, environment and human health and well-being of communities, through land-grant colleges and partner organizations. NIFA Funding should be increased and allocated to ensure a Local Food Extension agent is placed in each county in each state. North Carolina has already done this successfully (https://localfood.ces.ncsu.edu/). This is important because since the 1940s, extension agents have shifted their focus from small-scale sustainable agriculture to an industrial, commodity production, food system model. Creating Local Food Agents is a symbolic gesture to shifting attention to the importance of creating local, small-scale, sustainable food systems. These agents can assist communities in

local food trainings, infrastructure development, distribution and aggregation, marketing, education, nutrition awareness, preparation and consumption, and healthy food access.

- *City and Regional Planners*—Create policy tools and trainings for city and regional planners so that local food and access to local food is part of the built environment, and intentional planning of communities.
- *Local Food Policy Councils*—Create local food policy councils in communities with representation from all members of the community (including food insecure/food desert residents) that develop and enact policies that connect consumers with local food and local farmers.
- *Corner Store Initiatives*—Develop and support bipartisan state and local legislation that seeks to ensure healthy food options for food desert residents so that accessing healthy food at corner and convenience stores is a viable option. These initiatives across communities in the United States, such as in North Carolina (http://www.ncleg.net/Sessions/2015/Bills/House/PDF/H250v2.pdf), provide exemplars of ways to make meaningful change in low income, low-resourced, food desert communities.
- *Community Gardens*—Create policy tools for local governments that can help break down barriers that prevent allocation of green spaces and community opportunities for community gardens that benefit everyone. Urban farming and community gardens have enabled individuals to participate in growing food together. When individuals come together to participate in growing food together, preparing food together, and eating food together, distinctions between "givers" and "receivers" present in many hunger relief programs do not exist. National leading examples include Growing Power (http://www.growingpower.org/).
- *Food Justice/Food Sovereignty Movement*—Identify mechanisms and funding streams to bring together food justice and food sovereignty leaders and projects across the nation to create a national learning community for successful community food project leaders to share ideas and best practices. Document economic benefits in communities that have begun the systems-change work required to transform their local, community food system which benefits all members of their community, regardless of socioeconomic status, and ensures everyone has access to healthy food.

Key Resources

Bolen, Ed, Dottie Rosenbaum, Stacey Dean, and Brynne Keith-Jennings. 2016. "More Than 500,000 Adults Will Lose SNAP Benefits in 2106 as Waivers Expire." Center on Budget and Policy Priorities. Retrieved March 23, 2016. http://www.cbpp.org/research/food-assistance/more-than-500000-adults-will-lose-snap-benefits-in-2016-as-waivers-expire

Coleman-Jensen, Alisha, Matthew P. Rabbitt, Christian Gregory, and Anita Singh. 2015. "Household Food Security in the United States in 2014." United States Department of Agriculture Economic Research Service Food Assistance and Nutrition Research Program. Retrieved March 23, 2016. http://www.ers.usda.gov/publications/err-economic-research-report/err194.aspx

Cornell University. "A Primer on Community Food Systems: Linking Food, Nutrition and Agriculture," Ithaca, NY: Cornell University. Retrieved March 23, 2016. http://www.farmlandinfo.org/primer-community-food-systems-linking-food-nutrition-and-agriculture

Hossfeld, Leslie, E. Brooke Kelly, Amanda Smith, and Julia F. Waity. 2015. "Towards Economies That Won't Leave: Utilizing a Community Food Systems Model to Develop Multi-Sector Sustainable Economies in Rural Southeastern North Carolina." Pp 241–266 in *Place Based Perspectives in Food in Society*, edited by Kevin Fitzpatrick and Don Willis, New York, NY: Palgrave MacMillan.

Feeding America http://www.feedingamerica.org/

Food Corps https://foodcorps.org/about

Food Policy Networks http://www.foodpolicynetworks.org/

Raja, Samina, Branden Born, and Jessica Kozlowski Russell. 2008. *A Planners Guide to Community and Regional Food Planning: Transforming Food Environments, Facilitating Healthy Eating (Report Number 554 Planning Advisory Service)*. Chicago, IL: American Planning Association.

Southeastern North Carolina Food Systems Program (Feast Down East) http://www.feastdowneast.org

USDA Economic Research Service. Food Access Research Atlas http://www.ers.usda.gov/data-products/food-access-research-atlas.aspx

About the Authors

Leslie Hossfeld, Ph.D. is Professor and Head of the Department of Sociology at Mississippi State University. Trained in Rural Sociology from North Carolina State University College of Agriculture and Life Sciences, Dr. Hossfeld has extensive experience in rural economic development and local food systems initiatives. She has made presentations to the United States Congress and the North Carolina Legislature on economic restructuring and rural economic decline. She was founding executive director of Feast Down East (www. feastdowneast.org) in Southeastern North Carolina and is currently co-founder and director of the Mississippi Food Insecurity Project (www. mfip.msstate.edu), which examines food access and food insecurity in Mississippi.

E. Brooke Kelly, Ph.D. is Professor of Sociology at the University of North Carolina at Pembroke, where she works with students and community partners on community-based research projects addressing poverty and food insecurity. Since her training at Michigan State University, her research has focused on social inequalities, work, and family, and more recently on food insecurity. Dr. Kelly has served as chair of the Poverty, Class, and Inequalities Division of the Society for the Study of Social Problems, chair of the Southern Sociological Society's committee on Sociological Practice, and as fellow and research affiliate of the Rural Policy Research Institute's Rural Poverty Center, researching rural low-income mothers' efforts to attain and maintain paid employment.

Julia Waity, Ph.D. is an Assistant Professor of Sociology at the University of North Carolina Wilmington. Dr. Waity's research focuses on poverty, food insecurity, and spatial inequality. She has presented her work at the American Sociological Association, the Society for the Study of Social Problems, the Southern Sociological Society, and the Research Innovation and Development Grants in Economics (RIDGE) Conference. Dr. Waity has received funding for her research from Indiana University, where she earned her Ph.D., the University of North Carolina Wilmington, and the Southern Rural Development Center.

FIVE

After Health Care Reform: Enduring Challenges for Justice in the American Health Care System

Jennifer Roebuck Bulanda

The Problem

Numerous sources, including the World Health Organization, Institute of Medicine, and the Commonwealth Fund, show that the U.S. spends more than any other developed nation on health care, but lags behind in terms of key health indicators such as life expectancy and infant mortality. Despite the high spending, U.S. citizens express lower satisfaction with their health care than those in other industrialized nations, and the U.S. is the only developed country that does not have a universal health care system. These shortcomings, coupled with steady growth in the number of uninsured and underinsured Americans, set the stage for the passage of the Patient Protection and Affordable Care Act (hereafter referred to as the ACA) in 2010. Although legislators aimed to solve a major social problem by making health care more accessible and affordable, early results suggest this intent has not been fully realized. The number of uninsured peaked at over 49 million in 2010, according to estimates by the U.S. Census Bureau. By 2015, a Kaiser Family Foundation (KFF) analysis shows this number had dropped to 32 million after passage and implementation of the ACA. Although a reduction in the number of uninsured is laudable, millions of Americans remain uninsured, and health care is still not considered a basic human right.

The ACA aimed to expand insurance coverage to more Americans through three main avenues: increasing employer responsibility, increasing individual responsibility, and increasing government responsibility. It also placed a number of restrictions on insurance companies, such as prohibiting consideration of pre-existing conditions and placing annual or lifetime limits on coverage. These changes have been beneficial in reducing the number of people who are uninsured and helping to ensure that Americans have more comprehensive coverage. However, recent evaluations of the legislation point to some enduring challenges. Estimates by KFF suggest that, of the 32 million people who remain uninsured, about half are either eligible for Medicaid or subsidies to aid them in purchasing insurance. Another 10 percent are individuals who fall into the Medicaid gap: they live in states that did not expand their Medicaid program, but have income too low to qualify for subsidies that would help them purchase insurance. Fifteen percent are undocumented immigrants, who are not eligible for Medicaid or subsidies to purchase insurance through the exchange. These issues and potential solutions are described in detail below.

The Research Evidence

The first key component of the ACA is an employer mandate, requiring employers with 50 or more employees to offer affordable insurance to employees or pay a penalty, and encouraging small businesses to offer insurance by providing tax incentives. The goal of the provision was to address the declining number of employees offered insurance through their employment, and the fact that employers who did offer insurance could offer policies with poor coverage and subsidize little or none of the cost. The employer mandate was delayed until 2016 for medium-sized businesses, making it difficult to fully assess the effectiveness of the provision at this point in time. There is some mixed evidence on the effect of the mandate on employment practices, with some anecdotal evidence suggesting employers are more likely to hold employees under the threshold for full-time work, thus not having to provide insurance benefits to them, and other research, such as a 2016 analysis of the Census Bureau's Current Population Survey published in *Health Affairs,* suggesting little evidence for such a trend.

The second key component of the ACA required those without insurance to purchase it from a private insurance company. This was notoriously difficult to do prior to the ACA, as insurance companies deny coverage to those with pre-existing conditions or exempt their condition from coverage. Purchase of insurance is now facilitated by creation of insurance "marketplaces" (or "exchanges") through which people without insurance from their employer can shop online for and purchase an insurance policy. Paying the entire cost of health insurance out of pocket is not viable for most people; therefore, just as employers generally subsidize their employees' health insurance premiums, the law provides subsidies on a sliding scale for Americans who make between 138 percent and 400 percent of the federal poverty line (FPL). In order to encourage people to sign up, a fine is levied on uninsured individuals who do not purchase a policy. However, these changes have not resulted in universal coverage for this population. Some people are exempt from the requirement to have insurance, such as those for whom insurance premiums would be over 8 percent of their household income and those with income below the threshold for filing income taxes. Undocumented immigrants are not eligible to purchase insurance through the marketplaces. Others choose not to purchase a policy and instead pay the penalty for not obtaining insurance; for some, this fine is cheaper than the cost of insurance.

The ACA also expanded the role of the government in ensuring that individuals with low income have insurance access. Prior to health care reform, eligibility for Medicaid (a governmental program designed to provide health insurance for individuals in poverty) varied widely from state to state; in some states, people at 125 percent of the FPL could access Medicaid, whereas in other states, individuals had to be at 50 percent of the FPL or lower. The ACA aimed to establish consistency in Medicaid eligibility, requiring that states expand their Medicaid coverage to all individuals within 138 percent of the FPL, and made income the only eligibility criterion for Medicaid access. However, in the first Supreme Court case challenging the legality of the ACA, the court ruled that the federal government could not withhold federal Medicaid funding to states if the states did not comply with the Medicaid expansion. This, in effect, made Medicaid expansion optional for states. As of January 2016, only 32 states have expanded their Medicaid programs. This has created a "Medicaid gap," in which some low-income individuals do not meet their state's Medicaid eligibility criteria, but are too poor to qualify for subsidies to buy their own policy through the exchanges, since subsidies are available only to those making between 100 percent and 400 percent of the FPL.

Finally, the ACA placed a number of restrictions on insurance companies, including prohibiting certain "junk policies" that provided very limited coverage, making lifetime or annual limits on coverage illegal, allowing young adults to stay on their parents' plan until age 26, mandating coverage for certain types of preventative care, and establishing baseline requirements (or "essential health benefits") that must be included in insurance coverage. These restrictions have allowed more people to access health care, but still have some shortcomings. One way in which insurance companies can offer lower monthly premiums is by offering high deductible plans. Research shows that individuals with such plans may be more likely to delay or avoid accessing health care due to the steep up front, out-of-pocket costs. In addition, constraints on insurance companies have translated to lower profit margins for some insurers on policies sold through the marketplaces. This has led some companies to cut back on the policies they offer or to even consider no longer offering plans through the marketplace. The effect on premiums since the ACA has gone into effect is mixed. Although average premiums for insurance purchased through the exchanges have risen overall, there is geographic variation due to the fact that insurance plans vary from state to state; in some geographic areas premiums have declined.

Recommendations and Solutions

As discussed above, the ACA has increased insurance coverage and provided more comprehensive coverage for millions of Americans, but also has some important limitations. There are several potential solutions for these problems, and the following represent areas in which social activists, even if they are not involved in policy making itself, can be influential:

1. Increase educational outreach opportunities and knowledge of the ACA among the American public, particularly for those who might benefit most from its provisions.

Recent polls show that many Americans are ill-informed about what the ACA entails and have low levels of health insurance literacy generally, including a lack of knowledge of programs such as Medicaid and the Child Health Insurance Program (CHIP). Recent studies by KFF found that, of the uninsured people who were eligible to purchase insurance through the marketplaces, only 34 percent had enrolled. Further, almost 90 percent of the uninsured were unaware of when the open enrollment period began for the marketplaces, two thirds reported knowing little or nothing about the health insurance marketplaces, and over half were unaware that subsidies are available to help people with low to moderate incomes purchase an insurance policy. Over 80 percent of those without insurance had not been contacted about health insurance opportunities or requirements within the past six months. This points to an important area for intervention.

Helping Americans understand the structure of the health care system and how to leverage insurance represents an opportunity for outreach efforts. These efforts are particularly important for groups that are less informed about the legislation and more likely to lack insurance, including those with lower levels of income and education, and race-ethnic minority groups such as blacks and Latinos. Advocacy efforts may be most effective when attentive to partnering with a broad coalition of stakeholders and organizations and offering outreach efforts in a broad variety of locations. For example, advocates can work in partnership with local schools, churches, libraries, and health centers in areas where uninsured populations are particularly high (for more in-depth examples, see publications of advocacy organizations such as Community Catalyst). Some grassroots organizations have sponsored sessions to train individuals who regularly come into contact with people who are uninsured (e.g., health care workers, clergy, staff at community agencies and food pantries), helping them to better understand the health care law and how to assist others in obtaining insurance. Creating advertising campaigns and printed materials (with attention to variations in language and education level) can also help to disseminate information, through, for example, canvassing door-to-door or posting flyers in target locations and distributing information at community events. Activists should consider partnering with organizations that have a vested interest in increasing insurance rates, such as hospitals and other health care facilities, and thinking creatively about other potential partnerships. For example, *The New York Times* profiled a service-learning program in Alabama (Bama Covered), in which university students were trained to go into the community and help with enrollment efforts. Sponsoring community sessions and setting up temporary enrollment locations that provide one-on-one help navigating the process of accessing the online marketplaces or signing up for Medicaid appear particularly beneficial. A recent Commonwealth Fund report finds that those who received personal assistance were significantly more likely to enroll in a marketplace plan than those who did not.

2. Address the Medicaid coverage gap.

The ACA intended to provide insurance to all individuals through a continuum of sources dependent on income. Individuals who do not receive insurance through an employer or some other program were supposed to receive it in one of three ways: those below 138 percent of the FPL were to receive insurance through Medicaid (which meant all states needed to expand eligibility to this cutoff), those between 138 percent and 400 percent of the FPL were to purchase insurance through the Exchanges with subsidies available to make it more affordable, and those with income above 400 percent of the FPL were to purchase it through the marketplace without subsidies. However, the decision of some states not to expand Medicaid has left a hole in this continuum of coverage. For example, an individual with income below 100 percent of the FPL living in a state that did not expand Medicaid would not be Medicaid-eligible, and would also not be eligible for subsidies to help purchase a policy through the marketplace, since the law stipulates that subsidies are reserved for those making between 100 percent and 400 percent of the FPL. This is a clear social justice issue; low-income individuals living in these states are left without options for accessing health insurance, as paying full premiums out of pocket is unreasonable given their income. In addition, Southern states have disproportionately chosen not to expand their Medicaid programs, and given the demographic composition of these states, this means lower-income black individuals are disproportionately affected.

One way to address this gap would be for the 18 states that have not yet expanded Medicaid to do so. Even if individual states continue to refuse Medicaid expansion, the gap could be attenuated if Congress were to modify the wording of the legislation to stipulate that anyone with income up to 400 percent of the FPL is eligible for subsidies, removing the minimum income threshold. Unfortunately, health care reform remains a highly politicized issue, one to which some politicians are ideologically opposed and others are fearful of political repercussions, which will likely continue to limit the expansion of Medicaid in some states. This is a main reason that advocacy efforts encouraging governors and legislators to approve Medicaid expansion have not been successful in all states. However, continued advocacy is vitally important. A number of diverse organizations, such as the National Health Law Program, Center on Budget and Policy Priorities, Families USA, and NETWORK Lobby, provide online resources or toolkits for activists; there are also numerous online state-specific resources. Advocacy efforts may be most successful when working in conjunction with other stakeholders who would benefit from Medicaid expansion, such as hospitals and other health care providers. Activists can organize campaigns to encourage constituents to write letters to or meet with their legislators and Governor. They should also find ways to educate others about justice issues related to Medicaid expansion. Letters to the editor and social media posts represent opportunities to inform the broader public and increase the number of voices calling for Medicaid expansion.

3. Avoid further politicizing the issue.

More than five years following passage of the ACA, opinions about health care reform remain highly divided along partisan lines. A January 2016 KFF poll shows 44 percent of Americans reporting an unfavorable view of the legislation and 41 percent reporting a favorable view. However, when those with an unfavorable view of the overall legislation are asked about specific provisions of the law, such as insurance companies no longer being able to deny coverage for people with pre-existing conditions, support is much more favorable. This suggests that if Americans better understood the legislation, there may be more bipartisan support for it. Unfortunately, the legislation itself has often become a symbol of broader sentiments about political ideology rather than understood and judged on its own merits. The interpretation and enactment of the ACA provisions has been dynamic, constantly undergoing changes, and is likely to continue to do so after the 2016 Presidential election and any changes in the composition of Congress. Bipartisan efforts to improve rather than dismantle the ACA (as some politicians are currently advocating) could be spurred by grassroots efforts to raise awareness of the issue and rally the millions who might lose their coverage if the health care reform legislation were undone. Reverting to a system marked by higher rates of uninsured and poorer coverage undermines justice in health care access. Advocacy that educates the American public on the social problems inherent in the current health care system could lead to collective action that opposes politicians' use of health care reform as a wedge issue and positions the American people as key stakeholders in the debate on health care reform, challenging the current lobbying power of other stakeholders such as health insurance companies.

4. If the goal is to achieve universal coverage, consider changing the underlying design of the system itself.

Although health care reform did make changes to the system, it did not change the system's underlying structure. A look at health care systems around the world offers a number of alternate models for achieving universal coverage. A system of socialized medicine, such as that in the UK, utilizes taxes to provide health care to all without the need for a health insurance system. A single-payer system, such as that in Canada, provides a single, government-provided health insurance program for all citizens. Finally, a multi-payer, universal system such as that in Switzerland or Germany retains the role of private insurance companies, but constrains those companies to either be non-profit companies or to be unable to profit on basic care. Other developed countries have used these different strategies to achieve the same goal: universal coverage. The U.S. has a particularly novel health care system, in that it is a patchwork of different types of systems. How you access health care varies widely for Americans, based on social factors such as age and income. For example, older individuals tend to experience a single-payer system (the Medicare system), and the system for veterans mirrors socialized medicine. Health care reform via the ACA maintained this patchwork system, and arguably strengthened the role of private insurance companies by requiring uninsured individuals to purchase a policy from these businesses. Thus, as was the case prior to health care reform, the U.S. still has a non-universal, multi-payer system. A number of alternate options have been and continue to be proposed, including offering a public health insurance option to compete with the private insurance options, and the possibility of shifting to a universal, single-payer system, which has been the focus of some recent politicians' calls for "Medicare for all." The range of different options available for restructuring our health care system can make it difficult for citizens or legislators to coalesce around any one system. However, helping American citizens to better understand our current system and potential alternatives can open opportunities for informed debate about future changes to the health care system.

Key Resources

Artiga, Samantha, Robin Rudowitz, and Jennifer Tolbert. 2016. "Outreach and Enrollment Strategies for Reaching the Medicaid Eligible but Uninsured Population." Kaiser Family Foundation Issue Brief. Retrieved March 21, 2016. http://kff.org/medicaid/issue-brief/outreach-and-enrollment-strategies-for-reaching-the-medicaid-eligible-but-uninsured-population/

Blumenthal, David and Sara Collins. 2014. "Health Care Coverage under the Affordable Care Act – A Progress Report." *New England Journal of Medicine,* 371(3):275-281. Retrieved March 21, 2016. http://docs.house.gov/meetings/IF/IF02/20140731/102587/HHRG-113-IF02-20140731-SD008.pdf

Collins, Sara, Munira Gunja, Michelle Doty, and Sophie Beutel. 2015. "To Enroll or Not to Enroll? Why Many Americans Have Gained Insurance Under the Affordable Care Act While Others Have Not." The Commonwealth Fund. Retrieved March 21, 2016. http://www.commonwealthfund.org/~/media/files/publications/issue-brief/2015/sep/1837_collins_to_enroll_not_enroll_tb.pdf

Community Catalyst. 2014. *Connecting Consumers to Coverage: Mobilizing for Enrollment. The Promise of the Affordable Care Act.* Retrieved March 21, 2016. http://www.communitycatalyst.org/resources/publications/document/connecting-consumers-to-coverage.pdf

Garfield, Rachel and Anthony Damico. 2016. "The Coverage Gap: Uninsured Poor Adults in States that Do Not Expand Medicaid – An Update." Kaiser Family Foundation. Retrieved March 21, 2016. http://kff.org/health-reform/issue-brief/the-coverage-gap-uninsured-poor-adults-in-states-that-do-not-expand-medicaid-an-update/

Kaiser Family Foundation. 2013. "Summary of the Affordable Care Act." Retrieved March 21, 2016 (http://files.kff.org/attachment/fact-sheet-summary-of-the-affordable-care-act).

Majerol, Melissa, Vann Newkirk, and Rachel Garfield. 2015. "The Uninsured: A Primer - Key Facts about Health Insurance and the Uninsured in the Era of Health Reform." Retrieved March 21, 2016. http://kff.org/uninsured/report/the-uninsured-a-primer-key-facts-about-health-insurance-and-the-uninsured-in-the-era-of-health-reform/

New York Times. 2014. "Is the Affordable Care Act Working?" *The New York Times.* Retrieved March 21, 2016. http://www.nytimes.com/interactive/2014/10/27/us/is-the-affordable-care-act-working.html?_r=0#/

RAND. 2014. "A Health Care Puzzler." RAND Corporation Research Brief Series. Retrieved March 21, 2016. http://www.rand.org/content/dam/rand/pubs/research_briefs/RB9700/RB9782/RAND_RB9782.pdf

Reid, T. R. 2010. *The Healing of America: A Global Quest for Better, Cheaper, and Fairer Health Care.* New York: Penguin Books.

About the Author

Jennifer Roebuck Bulanda, Ph.D. is Associate Professor in the Department of Sociology and Gerontology at Miami University. Her research focuses on family relationships and their impact on health and well-being, particularly during the later life course. She regularly teaches courses that cover the U.S. health system, comparative perspectives on health care, Medicare and Medicaid, and health care reform. In one of her recent Medical Sociology courses, students completed a service-learning project in which they led a community education session on the Affordable Care Act and helped attendees without health insurance access the new insurance exchanges and assess their Medicaid eligibility.

SECTION III

Race, Labor, and Poverty

SIX

Global Labor Social Justice on University Campuses

Michelle Christian

The Problem

Hidden underneath many of our favorite brand labels is a garment worker's death, injury, or abuse. Examples are plentiful: on April 24, 2013 Rana Plaza in Bangladesh collapsed killing 1,134 apparel workers who supplied for Walmart, Sears and other brands. Just the year before in Dhaka, Bangladesh, 112 workers died in the Tazreen factory fire. Over 500 workers died, with thousands of injuries, in Bangladesh garment factories prior to the Rana Plaza collapse, including the Spectrum Sweater factory collapse killing 62 workers in 2005. The problem is widespread: in 2012, more than 300 apparel workers in Karachi, Pakistan, died in a global brand-audited company.

After 30 years of labor rights advocacy and critical scholarship on the global garment industry, we know that producing clothes to meet our insatiable consumer and fast-fashion demands has made the job of garment worker a dangerously precarious one, particularly for female workers. Recent academic scholarship and advocacy research document the prevalence of poverty wages and safety hazards for workers. The pervasiveness of hardship wages defines workers' struggles. According to the Clean Clothes Campaign and the Asia Floor Wage Alliance's 2014 report, poverty wages persist across six of the largest garment producing countries, and the minimum wage declined by 28 percent between 1998 and 2013. The problem is widespread: workers in Eastern European countries producing for Western European markets have an even larger gap between the low minimum and needed living wage. In addition to the unchanged low wages two years after the Rana Plaza disaster, according to the International Labor Rights Forum, fear, violence, intimidation, and retaliation are also commonplace. The Worker Rights Consortium found that Haitian garment workers, already working in the poorest country in the Western hemisphere, experience ubiquitous wage theft, causing dire consequences for families and communities.

Universities in the United States have emerged as key sites of social justice advocacy and policy action in response to the inadequate industry and government responses to garment factory deaths and extreme working conditions and wages. Student activists, in solidarity with garment workers' global mobilization efforts, have joined with faculty and administrator allies to use their leverage as key licensors of university logo goods to support worker rights and promote structural change in the industry. More action is needed to strengthen and build upon the work university stakeholders have begun in order to spread workers' ability to achieve dignified work with a living wage.

Research Evidence

There is a wealth of scholarship on the rise of vast apparel global value chains, the influence of neoliberal trade and development policies that fueled their growth, and how these chains have created a vulnerable gendered international division of labor. Apparel global value chains are highly fragmented between the stages of production and widely geographically distributed. As buyer-driven chains they are shaped and driven by large global retailers and branded marketers who set the standards and parameters that apparel suppliers in the global South must meet to produce for the global marketplace. Just-in-time production fueled by the emergence of fast fashion and an unpredictable consumer market requires quick production cycles, flexible agreements for buyers, and low price points. Thus, breaking up the production process through outsourcing, the "sweating system," and offshoring occurs all the way down to home-based work.

The globalization of apparel manufacturing emerged with the onset of neoliberal development policies demanded of global South countries by multilateral organizations. One outcome of these demands was the creation of export processing zones (EPZs) with limited taxes and environmental labor regulation benefiting foreign and national firms located there. Developing nations further used their abundant cheap labor to lure multinational firms. In addition, a free trade regime reinforced by neoclassical economic market logic supported the fragmentation and dispersion of production, resulting in production by global firms being subsidized through low cost labor. Thus, global firms did not have to pay the full price of meeting global labor standards, and essentially created a "race to the bottom" on labor costs for countries and factories attempting to compete.

These structural conditions produced vulnerable workers who continuously negotiated weak and precarious working conditions. Apparel manufacturing is labor intensive, dominated by female workers from rural regions with limited education. The gendering of apparel production was proactively created on shop floors when managers sought perceived docile, flexible labor to meet global demands, constructing the work as low-skill and unprotected by unions. Consequently, many female workers were subject to long hours, low pay, unsafe production conditions, and gender policing and harassment. By the late 1990s, advocacy groups like the National Labor Committee and the Clean Clothes Campaign joined with U.S. garment worker associations and unions, and United Students Against Sweatshops, and began highlighting the sweatshop conditions in which our clothes were produced. The industry was forced to respond.

The industry's response to accusations of sweatshop working conditions was to create a social compliance model of voluntary codes of conduct, subject to different forms of monitoring practices for suppliers. Different associations tasked with code oversight such as SA8000 (created by the private sector), Worldwide Responsible Apparel Production (created by American manufacturers), and Fair Labor Association (FLA) (a multi-stakeholder group including global brands) emphasize different standards and enforcement practices. Confusion over code content and requirements resulted, with limited labor rights enhancement. For example, three factories in Rana Plaza had been audited prior to the collapse, proving the weakness and limitations of the system. Monitoring has also not been universal. A 2014 Georgetown Alta Gracia study found that the FLA only audited 3.5 percent of contracted factories from member brands. There is broad agreement among scholars that the social compliance model has done little to improve the conditions of workers, especially around collective bargaining and freedom of association rights.

Recommendations and Solutions

As the social compliance model held sway, one institution emerged as a site for potential transformative change in the industry: the U.S. university. Universities and colleges in the U.S. have risen as powerful institutions demanding and implementing change in collegiate apparel global value chains, advocating on behalf of garment workers.

University licensed logo apparel is big business: collegiately licensed materials represent a $4.6 billion share in the retail market. The Collegiate Licensing Company, a company that assists 200 colleges (almost 80 percent of the market) in their licensee deals, has paid over $1.5 billion in royalties to clients since its inception in 1981. The biggest global athletic brands, Nike, Adidas, and Under Armour, all jockey to outfit top athletic departments at universities. In 2015, according to *Forbes,* Nike and the University of Michigan signed the most valuable apparel deal in college sports history, valued at $122.32 million for the years 2016-2027.

Clearly, universities represent a key consumer market for athletic and retail brands. Student activists have used this leverage to push their universities to hold licensee suppliers accountable for the working conditions found in their vast supply chains. Since 1998, the United Students Against Sweatshops (USAS) have protested against the conditions under which university apparel is produced. In waves of student sit-ins, administrative building occupations, and anti-sweatshop awareness campaigns, such as "I'd Rather Go Naked than Wear Sweatshop Clothes," student activists fought for stricter university codes of conduct, enforcement measures, and factory disclosure lists from licensees. USAS helped to establish the Worker Rights Consortium (WRC) as an alternative to the Fair Labor Association.

The establishment of the Worker Rights Consortium in 2000 was a milestone moment in shifting the status quo in how factories were monitored and how accountability and remediation was pursued after violations were found. Its uniqueness is found in its governance structure, which includes university representatives, labor rights experts, and USAS representatives, and in the fact that the WRC investigates worker complaints of abuses. There are 184 colleges and universities affiliated to the WRC. These universities require their licensees to disclose all of their supplier factory locations and meet the university's code of conduct. The WRC maintains a database of factory inspection and remediation reports and issues advice and communiques to universities about code violations, notifying them if corrective action to licensee supplier violations was or was not taken. The WRC also played a role in supporting the founding of Alta Gracia, a factory built upon the idea that high labor standards and global apparel production is possible.

Alta Gracia was founded in 2010 in the Dominican Republic as a model collegiate apparel factory. Forming from a partnership between labor rights advocates, student activists, and Joe Bozich, then CEO of Knights Apparel, Alta Gracia workers receive a *salario digno,* a living wage 350 percent higher than the country's minimum wage, in addition to other worker protections around safety, medical care, and collective bargaining. Alta Gracia sales registered $11 million in 2013 and continue to grow, proving that fair working conditions can be a model for apparel factory success. Still, Alta Gracia is only one factory in the greater apparel manufacturing community. The fact that greater labor challenges abound in the sector was made poignant with the Rana Plaza collapse three years after Alta Gracia was formed. In the tragedy's wake, however, a potential industry-changing agreement emerged with the Accord on Fire and Building Safety in Bangladesh. Universities played a significant role in pushing its adoption.

The Accord on Fire and Building Safety in Bangladesh is a legally binding contract between global brands/retailers and international unions that prioritizes worker representation and brand responsibility in its governance structure and mandates. Notably, it fills common regulatory gaps found in the existing social compliance monitoring model, and makes structural changes in the dominant sourcing model. Provisions require enforcing independent inspections for all factory suppliers, including sub-contracts; requiring brands to provide financial assistance for factory safety; and requiring brands to commit to long-term, stable sourcing agreements. If brand responsibility is not met in the timetable for remediation, factories are subject to binding arbitration. Over 200 brands and retailers from 20 countries signed the Accord. Under the WRC's recommendation, more than 25 universities have demanded that licensees that sourced, produced, or purchased collegiate apparel in Bangladesh as of January 2013 sign the Accord.

Even with these accomplishments, more is needed at the university level. There are several actions universities can pursue to further strengthen garment worker rights and solidify the university as an institution of global social justice. USAS students and other progressive student organizations have worked tirelessly to hold their universities to the high standards they espouse. The following recommendations have been articulated by students and others pushing their universities to be socially just consumers of the products of the global garment industry.

1. Strengthen the Accord on Fire and Building Safety in Bangladesh.

Two and a half years after the Rana Plaza tragedy, more than 1,300 factories were inspected, 1,160 Corrective Action Plans (CAPs) were developed, more than 650 follow-up inspections were conducted, and tens of thousands of individual building repairs were made. A level of laudable transparency in disseminating Accord inspection information publicly to workers was achieved. Still, the Accord, the WRC, and other advocacy groups are troubled at the pace of remediation, with thousands of factories lagging behind designated deadlines. The WRC reports that some Accord signatory brands are not living up to their obligations. In collaboration with the Clean Clothes Campaign, International Labor Rights Forum (ILRF), and the Maquila Solidarity Network, WRC found that 52 percent of H&M's (Bangladesh's biggest apparel buyer) top suppliers are behind schedule in fire safety repairs providing workers' escape. The urgency of needed repairs became all the more apparent when on February 2, 2016 a fire broke out at the Matrix Sweaters Factory, a supplier for H&M and other brands like Walmart and Gap. Although no loss of life occurred, workers could have been trapped if the fire had occurred a few hours later.

Universities can continue to support the Accord by making their licensees in Bangladesh become signatories, if they are not already, and by highlighting the challenges that the Accord still faces from brand remediation stalling even if they are not direct licensees. Universities can send communiques to their licensees that they are proactively following Accord updates and that they expect them to meet all of their Accord commitments. This pressure tactic shows licensees that universities are active participants with the Accord process. Furthermore, as Accord participants with the WRC, universities can address the continued need for industry change by highlighting the areas the Accord is not covering, such as wages and gender-based inequalities, and considering how to expand Accord practices beyond factories producing for signatory brands. The ILRF report argues that we need to move beyond a technical, engineering-based definition of safety to include workers' own understanding and perspective, which encapsulates mutual respect and dignity of work and voice. That dignity includes higher wages; the average Bangladeshi wage of U.S. $68 a month continues to be the lowest in the world and traps workers in cycles of overlapping hardships. Factories that are not signatories of the Accord inspection unit continue to use fear, violence, and intimidation as tools of repression against worker organizing. Issues specific to women, such as rampant gendered policing, lack of attention to reproductive health access, and voice, need to be brought to the forefront in what Law on the Margin calls a workers' rights program through a gender lens. Universities must contribute to this pressure.

2. Implement a designated supplier program.

The Accord represents a paradigm shift in brand accountability but is only applied in one country. A way to expand the principles of the Accord and also widen standards would be for universities to initiate the WRC-suggested Designated Supplier Program (DSP). A DSP program requires licensees to source a percentage of university apparel from factories that meet a series of high labor standards that are independently verified. The paradigm shifting potential of the DSP is found in the licensee obligations to their suppliers. Licensees would be required to pay a fair price standard to factories to cover the true cost of meeting high labor standards, and to commit to production agreements of no less than three years, which commit a minimum volume of orders to their DSP factories. Part of the key labor standard would be a commitment for factories to pay a living wage based upon country and region determinants. Moreover, factories would have to show their respect and support for freedom of association and potential trade unionization. Enforcement and transparency mechanisms are also built into the program. In signing up for the DSP, universities would unequivocally show their commitment to worker social justice. The DSP moves beyond a piecemeal approach to ethical sourcing and or reactionary policies emergent from global tragedies. Demonstrating that a certain percentage of their sourced apparel goods are produced with the highest commitment to human rights, universities could shape the larger industry and show that it is not only possible but ethically necessary to change how global actors hold themselves accountable for labor injustices in their supply chains.

3. Strengthen Alta Gracia as a model for other factories.

Universities can also commit larger orders to Alta Gracia produced apparel and supply marketing resources to promote the brand on campus. The success of Alta Gracia can pave the way for implementation of the DSP by demonstrating the success of ethically sourced goods. To date, Alta Gracia is still the only independently verified living wage collegiate garment factory in the Global South, but it sets the standard global factories should meet. University outlets should also help support Alta Gracia and work collaboratively with the brand as it grows and tries to meet the demands of collegiate apparel while combatting the poor working conditions so common in the sector. Faculty can also offer their classrooms as a learning laboratory on the difficulties associated with apparel production, and show how students can actively get involved in global justice campaigns through promoting Alta Gracia and DSP on campus.

4. Hold the largest licensees to the highest standard of ethical sourcing.

Top athletic brands pour millions of dollars into university athletics, but their financial power should not preclude them from meeting the demands of university codes of conduct and allowing the universities' monitoring agents access to their factories. In Fall 2015, Nike decided not to provide specific factory disclosure information to universities and their licensing agents and refused to grant the WRC access to their factories for university monitoring. Nike made inroads after activists documented abuses and has worked with the WRC in the past, but this is a step backwards. USAS initiated a campaign across 30 campuses to demand that their schools force Nike to allow WRC access.

Universities have something that Nike and other top global athletic brands want: athletes, students, and fans to wear their gear. There are few global actors that can pressure these brands like universities can. In a context where brand endorsements are getting larger and universities look for revenue sources beyond the state, it is imperative that universities stand firm when code violations occur. Athletics departments should also play a role. Non-paid student athletes become the brand ambassadors for these billion-dollar companies. These athletes can become a different type of brand ambassador, one for ethically produced goods, fair treatment, and social justice.

Key Resources

Bair, Jennifer, Marsha A. Dickson, and Doug Miller, eds. 2014. *Workers' Rights and Labor Compliance in Global Supply Chains: Is a Social Label the Answer?* New York: Routledge.

Dicken, Peter. 2011. *Global Shift: Mapping the Changing Contours of The World Economy.* 6th Ed. New York: Guilford Press.

Esbenshade, Jill. 2004. *Monitoring Sweatshops: Workers, Consumers, and the Global Apparel Industry.* Philadelphia, PA: Temple University Press.

Featherstone, Lisa. 2002. *Students Against Sweatshops.* New York: Verso.

Fernández-Kelly, María Patricia. 1983. *For We Are Sold, I and My People: Women and Industry in Mexico's Frontier.* Albany: State University of New York Press.

Gereffi, Gary and Miguel Korzeniewicz. 1994. *Commodity Chains and Global Capitalism.* Westport, ct: Praeger.

International Labor Rights Forum. 2015. "Our Voices, Our Safety Bangladeshi Garment Workers Speak Out."

Kline, John and Edward Soule. 2014. "Alta Gracia: Four Years and Counting." Research Results Report, Reflective Engagement Initiative, Georgetown University. http://ignatiansolidarity.net/wp-content/uploads/2014/08/AltaGracia-LowRes-1.pdf

Law at the Margins http://lawatthemargins.com Law at the Margins uses social media to highlight the ways our laws and legal institutions expand or limit the rights and social justice aspirations of people and communities.

Workers Rights Consortium (WRC) http://www.workersrights.org WRC is an independent labor rights monitoring organization, conducting investigations of working conditions in factories around the globe.

About the Author

Michelle Christian, Ph.D. is an Assistant Professor in the Department of Sociology at the University of Tennessee-Knoxville. Her research focuses on the intersection of race and gender inequalities in the global economy, most notably by examining forms of precarious, service-based work. Between 2010 and 2013 she was a sector coordinator for, Capturing the Gains, an international research program that explored the contours to economic and social upgrading in global production networks. She has conducted fieldwork in Costa Rica, Kenya, Uganda, and the United States, and oversaw fieldwork in Indonesia, South Africa, and India.

SEVEN

When Home Disappears: How the Rise in Urban Foreclosures and Evictions Threatens Families

Obie Clayton and Barbara Harris Combs

The Problem

Since the housing crisis of 2008 and recession of 2009, the realities of poverty and housing in American society have changed dramatically. In fact, changes to housing policies in the decades prior to the recession (touted as urban renewal) resulted in many poor and low income households either being pushed out of the city or forced to dedicate more of their income for housing. Constraints on affordable housing have never been greater. In 2009, Atlanta, which was the first city to erect public housing, announced it would become the first city to demolish its public housing. By 2011 the process was complete. Other cities followed suit. Hope IV and other federal policies also contributed to the shortage of affordable housing in the city. Today, housing evictions are on the rise. This is because the problem of affordable housing in the city is pressing, so pressing in fact, that evictions are no longer rare.

Rising rents, stagnant incomes, and limited public housing assistance combined to form a perfect storm creating our current affordable housing crisis. Throughout much of the 1990s median asking rents rose at a rate consistent with increases in income; however, in the 2000s the median asking rate for rent soared nationwide. In the southern U.S. rents rose about 20 percent, but in parts of the northeast it went up almost 40 percent. While the trend of rising rents can be traced back to the early 2000s, it shows no sign of dropping. The Portland Oregon Community Alliance of Tenants called 2015 "The summer of evictions." *The San Francisco Chronicle* reported a similar crisis, but the problem of rising evictions is not limited to the west coast. In 2014,

CNN reported that both rents and evictions were "soaring." Rents nationwide grew by 7 percent while incomes have remained relatively stagnant. The same CNN report stated one in five renter households in Georgia received an eviction notice during 2014.

When families are evicted there are many and multidimensional losses. Certainly there is a loss of home and physical possessions, but there is potentially a loss of community and emotional well-being. Children may lose their school. Eviction compromises many things— emotional, economic, and social psychological.

Home is a necessity for all, but for poor and working class Americans, housing comes at a very high cost. Because minorities are disproportionately likely to be poor, this has a particularly deleterious impact on black and Latino families. Matthew Desmond's 2015 report for the Institute for Research on Poverty outlines how forced evictions impact mothers. The consequences include poor health of the children, poor health for the mother, and increased risk of depression, parenting stress and material hardship. There is clear evidence that keeping families in their homes has the potential to mitigate some of the deleterious effects of urban inequality.

The Research Evidence

The 2013 American Housing Survey noted that while owner-occupants' costs fell during the period from 2011 to 2013, the costs paid by renters increased. According to the same survey, the poor often spend 50 percent to 70 percent of their income on housing costs. That percentage is unsustainable. Families are forced to secure all their other needs—food, clothing, medical expenses, heating/ air, transportation, dental, etc.—on the remaining 30 to 50 percent. At best, it is a prescription for remaining in poverty. At worst, it is a formula for eviction. Desmond, in a report published by The Institute for Research on Poverty, reported that over one million families spend over 70 percent of their income on housing and associated costs.

Racial and ethnic minorities are disproportionately likely to live in poverty. The 2013 American Housing Survey found that 23 percent of African American and 25 percent of Latino families spent at least half of their income on rent. We examined foreclosures in the Metro Atlanta area between 2007 and 2008 and found that almost 70,000 homes were foreclosed upon. As the data in Figure 1 illustrates, racial divides are evident, as is the correlation between high foreclosure rates and a high percentage of Black or Hispanic residents.

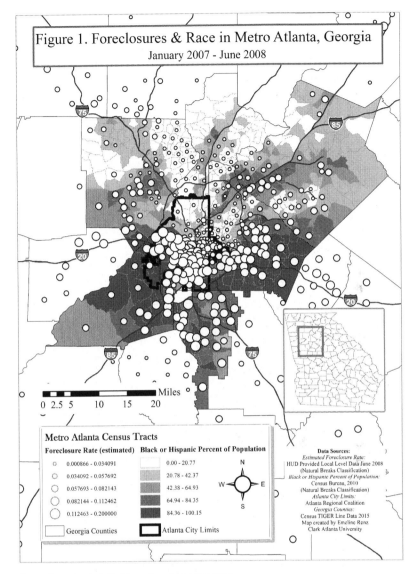

Figure 1. Foreclosures & Race in Metro Atlanta, Georgia
January 2007 - June 2008

Source: Created on behalf of the authors by Emeline Renz.

In addition to a lack of affordable housing, many Americans face the loss of their homes through foreclosure or eviction. This point has been stressed by many, including a report released by Occupy our Homes, a non profit group in Atlanta. Poor and low-income households are the most heavily impacted by foreclosures. This economically vulnerable population may reside in a property that is about to be foreclosed upon. Renters in foreclosed properties may be evicted with very limited notice. Under these forced circumstances, lower-income families are often forced to move to less favorable neighborhoods. Additionally, a majority of states are non-judicial foreclosure states (although some are handled as trustee sales), which means the lender can foreclose without going to court.

Many studies focus on foreclosures for two important reasons. First, foreclosure data is more readily available than data on evictions. Another reason that foreclosure data can be instructive is that according to 2010 Census files, only 63 percent of residential property is owner occupied. According to a 2014 Global Research Report, from January 2007 to December 2011 there were *more than four million completed foreclosures* and *more than 8.2 million foreclosure starts.* Many of these foreclosed properties were in Black and/or low-income neighborhoods. A significant number of these houses were taken over by hedge funds and investors, such as Blackstone. Invitation Homes, Blackstone's rental property division, had total assets of about $9 billion in 2015. No other property investment firm in the nation has as large a presence in the real estate industry as Blackstone. Such a position is dangerous. It not only provides great potential for renters to be taken advantage of in the market, but it also concentrates real estate wealth in a way that makes Blackstone and other similar investors "too big to fail." We saw that with the bailout of the nation's largest banks at the hands of the taxpayers.

When property investors are taken as a collective, they are in the position of buying houses so quickly that first time home buyers and renters are often pushed to the side. Further, these corporate investors have primarily been focusing their buying in cities that were devastated by the housing market collapse, such as Phoenix, Las Vegas, Chicago, Seattle, Tampa, Miami, Los Angeles, and Atlanta. Nationwide, more than 20 percent of properties in foreclosure are rentals, according to a December 2015 study by the National Low Income Housing Coalition. The study also says rentals are typically multi-family dwellings and that renters constitute about 40 percent of all families facing eviction.

In Atlanta, Georgia, the organization Occupy Our Homes Atlanta, released a report entitled *Blackstone: Atlanta's Newest Landlord,* which revealed that: "(1) Tenants wishing to stay in their homes can face automatic rent increases as much as 20 percent annually; (2) Survey participants living in homes owned by Invitation Homes pay nearly $300 more in rent than the Metro Atlanta median; (3) 45 percent of survey participants pay more than 30 percent of their income on rent, by definition making the rent unaffordable; (4) Tenants face high fees, including a $200 late fee for rental payments; and (5) 78 percent of the surveyed tenants do not have consistent or reliable access to the landlord or property manager." Similar findings are reported in other cities such as Milwaukee, San Francisco, and New York.

When a property is foreclosed upon, the occupants of the home—whether owner occupiers or renters—are impacted. So, whether by way of foreclosure or eviction deleterious outcomes result when home disappears.

Recommendations and Solutions

As is the case with many social problems, the issues here are complex and related to other social issues. As a result, policy recommendations should address the three problems we identify: (1) rising rents; (2) stagnant incomes; (3) decreased public housing assistance, but the foreclosure crisis is an important contributing factor to all of these.

The housing crisis affects all Americans. As a result, we need solutions that speak to the problems faced across and within income groups.

1. Non-judicial foreclosures should be stopped.

The enormous surge in rents affects everyone. Incomes for the bottom quintile of society have remained flat, and while there have been increases in income for other groups, it has remained small. Many renting families below the poverty line receive no housing assistance at all.

2. Housing assistance must be increased.

One of the less frequently discussed outcomes of rising housing foreclosures is that housing is being concentrated into the hands of fewer and fewer individuals. As corporations and small investors buy up the foreclosed housing stock in the inner city—often for the purpose of renting it out—tax incentives should be made available to those who agree to allow current renting occupants to remain (at the current rate) for the lease period and a one-year period beyond.

3. We need financial incentives to aid responsible landlords.

The eviction process is started by a landlord (or his or her representative). A number of landlords may lack the integrity, patience, or have the economic wherewithal to go through the formal eviction process. As a result, there are likely more evictions than the official records suggest. These landlords should also be required to enter into a bond or surety pledge against carrying out any forced evictions. If a tenant is able to prove a forced eviction, the bond would be forfeited.

We have discussed the fact that additional funding is needed, such as housing allowances, but making funds available does not mean people will avail themselves of the programs.

4. Trust needs to be restored between the American people, particularly disadvantaged populations, and our social institutions and service providers.

While a wide variety of people may be subjected to an eviction in their lifetime, certain groups are more likely to be evicted. Because a disproportionate number of poor Americans belong to ethnic and racial minority groups, and these groups tend to have higher levels of distrust of police and other service providers, credit counseling and other services aimed at targeted groups (like the National Urban League's Foreclosure Prevention and Education program) should also be funded. A related trust issue is:

5. We have to stop criminalizing eviction.

As public housing benefits began to shrink, the requirements to take advantage of those benefits became harder and harder to fulfill. Evictions have a wide range of effects. Often, an eviction may go on a person's "permanent record" just like a criminal charge, and down the road this can prevent the person from receiving public housing benefits. As a result, those who need help the most are foreclosed from receiving it. This is a dangerous precedent. Instead of housing being a right, it seems to instead suggest that some poor are deserving poor while others are not. In this way, forced evictions lead renters to say yes to substandard housing. This drop in neighborhood quality is problematic.

6. We need a housing bill of rights!

Finally, we think it is important for America to acknowledge that the homeownership model is neither tenable nor should it be desirable for masses of people. As a result, we need to: (1) make it a national priority to protect the rights of renters, and (2) recognize housing as a human right.

In his book *Evicted*, sociologist Matthew Desmond reports several important findings with respect to negotiating a successful outcome (i.e., a stipulation or dismissal) in evictions court. First, he found that those represented by counsel tended to fare better than those unrepresented. Second, he found that the presence of children is highly predictive of tenants being evicted.

Since the housing crisis, the Department of Housing and Urban Development (HUD) has made efforts to stabilize housing, especially in neighborhoods with a high proportion of foreclosures. Some homes available through the Neighborhood Stabilization Program (NSP) offer incentives (a First Look) to homebuyers, and if they are not sold during that period then they become available to others, including investors. We assert that the homeownership model is neither tenable nor should it be a goal for all. We suggest that incentives be made available to investors who agree to provide quality affordable homes to renters and maintain the property as such for a period of no less than five years. Stabilizing rents should be the new HUD model for stabilizing neighborhoods. Without such a practice, we fear that more and more homes will disappear, especially for the most vulnerable among us.

Key Resources

Call, Rob with Denechia Powell and Sarah Heck. 2014. "Blackstone Atlanta's Newest Landlord: The New Face of the Rental Market." Occupy our Homes. http://homesforall.org/wp-content/uploads/2014/04/BlackstoneReportFinal0407141.pdf

Desmond, Matthew. 2015. "Unaffordable America: Poverty, Housing, and Eviction." *Fast Focus, Institute for Research on Poverty*, 22:1-6.

Desmond, Matthew and Rachel Tolbert Kimbro. 2015. "Eviction's Fallout: Housing, Hardship, and Health." *Social Forces*, 94(1):295-324.

Desmond, Matthew and Tracey Shollenberger. 2015. "Forced Displacement from Rental Housing: Prevalence and Neighborhood Consequences." *Demography*, 52:1751-1772.

Desmond, Matthew, Weihua An, Richelle Winkler, and Thomas Ferris. 2013. "Evicting Children." *Social Forces*, 92:303-327.

Fraser, James C. and Deirdre Oakley. 2015. "The Neighborhood Stabilization Program: Stable for Whom?" *Journal of Urban Affairs*, 37:(1):38-41.

Hankins, Katherine, Mechele Puckett, Deirdre Oakley and Erin Ruel. 2014. "Forced Mobility: The Relocation of Public Housing Residents in Atlanta." *Environment and Planning A*, 46:2932-2949.

HUD. 2010. Neighborhood Stabilization Program data. *HUD Provided Neighborhood Level Foreclosure Data.* http://www.huduser.org/portal/datasets/nsp.html

Joint Center for Housing Studies of Harvard University. 2013. The State of the Nation's Housing 2013 4-5 (2013). http://www.jchs.harvard.edu/files/son2013.pdf

Kalil, Ariel and Patrick Wrightman. 2009. "Parental Job Loss and Children's Educational Attainment in Black and White Middle Class Families." National Poverty Center Working Paper Series #09-02. National Poverty Center. http://www.npc.umich.edu/publications/working_papers/?publication_id=171&

Marge, Martin, Steffen L. Barry, David A. Vandenbroucke, Yung Gann David Yao, Keith Fudge, and Maria Teresa Souza. 2011. *Worst Case Housing Needs 2009: Report to Congress.* Washington, DC: U.S. Department of Housing and Urban Development, Office of Policy Development and Research.

National Low Income Housing Coalition. 2015. "Out of Reach 2015: Low Wages and High Rents Lock Renters Out." http://nlihc.org/sites/default/files/oor/OOR_2015_FULL.pdf

About the Authors

Obie Clayton, Ph.D. is Professor and Chair of the Sociology and Criminal Justice Department at Clark Atlanta University in Atlanta, Georgia. Clayton has been studying urban inequality since the 1980s and was a member of former President Jimmy Carter's The Atlanta Project; a project designed to empower the poor in Atlanta. He has also received funding from the Russell Sage Foundation to examine housing discrimination in Atlanta. The results of this study have been published in David L. Sjoquist's edited volume, *The Atlanta Paradox,* a book that examines the substantial racial segregation in a community with a reputation for good race relations and of high inner-city poverty in the face of substantial economic growth.

Barbara Harris Combs, Ph.D. is an Associate Professor of Sociology and Criminal Justice at Clark Atlanta University in Atlanta Georgia. She received a doctoral dissertation research grant from the Department of Housing and Urban Development (HUD) to conduct post-recession research on two black gentrifying neighborhoods in Atlanta, Georgia, and she continues that work today as part of a collaborative research team with researchers at the University of South Carolina. Their work has been funded by NSF. She is also a member of the Persistent Poverty Project sponsored by the Southern Sociological Society.

EIGHT

The Racial Implications of Immigration Policy

Trenita B. Childers and San Juanita García

The Problem

Immigration policies shape how immigrants and their children are integrated into the United States. Much of the immigration debate is centered on claims to "fix the immigration problem." Conservative politicians propose enforcement policies, including mass deportations and the continued militarization of the U.S.-Mexico border as viable solutions. Importantly, these enforcement policies are concealed under a legal framework that criminalizes immigrants. While such policies are deemed "race-neutral," they disproportionately disenfranchise immigrant communities of color. Given these consequences, it is critical to disentangle and problematize colorblind conceptions in immigration policies.

We critically examine how social policies that may seem race-neutral actually target specific racial groups. Racial implications of policies must be brought to the forefront to ensure equitable treatment under the law. In an effort to "crack down" on undocumented immigrants in the United States, two specific types of policies have been enacted: extended policing authority and birthright citizenship policies. Both have repercussions that impact specific racial groups.

Policies that extend policing authority broaden the power of immigration enforcement from migration authorities to federal and local law enforcement officials. Importantly, this historic shift adds another layer to the ways that communities of color are policed—the pipeline to deportation supplements the existing pipeline to prison. Examples of this type of law include section 287(g) of the Immigration and Nationality Act, which allows the Department of Homeland Security to deputize selected state and local law enforcement officers to perform the functions of federal immigration agents. A more explicit policy, SB1070 in Arizona, *requires* state and local law enforcement agencies to check the immigration status of individuals they encounter. When each of these laws move from policy to practice, they result in the racial profiling of Latinos/as and harassment based on physical appearance.

Another set of policies challenge birthright citizenship, attacking the constitutional right to citizenship for those born in the U.S. to undocumented parents. Several counties in Texas, for example, have enacted policies that impede a parent's access to their child's birth certificate if parents cannot present adequate documentation. These policies actively target those perceived to be from Mexico as well as their U.S.-born children. In the past, undocumented parents could present a foreign ID such as the *matrícula consular* card as proof of identification to obtain birth certificates for their U.S.-born children. The decision to stop accepting this particular card in certain administrative locations specifically disadvantages Mexican immigrants and their families, and effectively creates generations of social exclusion on the basis of their race.

This chapter provides research evidence of the historical connection between immigration policies and race in the U.S. to give context to today's colorblind policies that impact particular racial groups. By focusing on immigration policies that have extended policing authority to law enforcement officials and challenged birthright citizenship to U.S.-born children of undocumented immigrants, this chapter shows that "race-neutral" immigration policies do indeed target particular racial groups. We conclude with recommendations and solutions for how to mitigate and eradicate racism in current immigration policies.

The Research Evidence

Defining Race

Race is an integral part of the lived experiences of people of color. Racial categories are defined by social experiences. Interactions with people and institutions affirm and solidify racial identities. While there is no biological basis for racial classification, people are often sorted into racial groups based on their physical characteristics, including skin color, facial features, and hair texture. Although people increasingly choose categories outside the given system (as evidenced by the "multiracial" and "other" categories), immigrants to the U.S. and their descendants are typically incorporated into existing racial categories:

Black, white, Asian, Latino. Nigerians and their descendants, for example, become black based on social interactions with the U.S. system of racial identification. Mexicans and their descendants become Latina/o.

As these categories become publicly disputed in the competition for different forms of power, race not only distinguishes between racial groups, it also promotes a hierarchy. Racial hierarchies are maintained by systems that privilege whiteness over other racial groups in the distribution of power, prestige, and resources. This inequitable system uses concepts like the American Dream, individualism, and meritocracy to bolster claims that colorblindness fosters equality.

Immigration policy has a long history of incorporating race—implicitly or explicitly—in its implementation. Operation Wetback offers one example of the explicit integration of race and immigration policy. In 1954, the Eisenhower administration instituted a military-style mass deportation initiative that resulted in broken families, human rights violations, and deaths. The goal of the deportation program was to secure the U.S.-Mexico border and deter undocumented immigration to the U.S. To this end, Operation Wetback targeted and deported over one million Mexican immigrants, many of whom were recruited to the United States to work in agriculture under the Bracero Program created in 1942. U.S.-born Mexican Americans were also deported through Operation Wetback. This highlights the murky divide between "true" Americans and people of color who are ultimately regarded as perpetual foreigners.

An examination of citizenship laws also reveals the historical integration of race and policy. The legal dividing line has typically been drawn at the "white/non-white" boundary. The key objective was to determine who had access to white rights and who did not. For example, whiteness was a prerequisite for American citizenship from 1790 until 1952. Therefore, many citizenship cases sought to determine whether certain populations - like Chinese, Hawaiian, Armenian, and Syrian ethnic groups - were considered white by law. This regulation of citizenship was race-based until the Hart-Celler Act of 1965 was passed during the civil rights era. Although this legislation marked an important shift away from overtly racist immigration policies, it also marked a shift towards the "race-neutral" and colorblind policies in effect today.

Contemporary legal and social discourses on immigration espouse colorblindness. Under the auspices of colorblindness, behaviors and practices are centered on the idea that we can create and enforce the law without seeing race. The corollary to this idea is that by being "blind" to race, all people are treated equally. However, since white privilege has always been a cornerstone of U.S. citizenship, it will continue to be a factor in our legal system's structures and practices.

In many ways, the effects of today's immigration policies mirror those of past decades, even while applying the language and principles of colorblindness. Present-day practices continue to marginalize and exclude particular racial groups. Although colorblind policies mask racism, they do not eliminate it. When overtly racist policies are dismantled, their vestiges continue to permeate the lives of targeted groups in new forms, thereby solidifying continued racial discrimination. As such, immigration policies must be examined to identify covert institutional mechanisms that disadvantage non-whites.

Race in Extended Policing Policies

Contemporary immigration policies negatively impact communities of color, namely Mexicans and other Latinas/os, through extended policing policies and the "poli-migra" enforcement regime. The "poli-migra" refers to the interconnections and multi-layered enforcement practices taking place at the federal, state, and local level laws and ordinances. Historically, with the Immigration Act of 1891, the U.S. federal government controlled the inspection and admission of immigrants. They were free to bar and exclude people they deemed "not desirable." This law created the Superintendent of Immigration, currently housed within the Department of Homeland Security under three bureaus: Customs and Border Patrol (CBP), Immigration and Customs Enforcement (ICE), and U.S. Citizenship and Immigration Services (USCIS).

Today, specific racial groups are targeted under a mass deportation regime. Indeed, under President Obama's administration we have seen some of the highest numbers of deportations, earning him the moniker "Deporter in Chief." Recent estimates reveal that over two million people have been deported under his administration. Furthermore, estimates from a 2014 report published by the U.S. Department of Homeland Security suggest that approximately 662,000 immigrants were apprehended in 2013, of which 64 percent were Mexican natives; and approximately 438,000 immigrants were deported, of which 72 percent were Mexican natives. In five years, the Obama administration deported about as many immigrants as George W. Bush's administration had deported in eight years.

Recent deportations have been facilitated by an increased level of enforcement activities by local police officers. Specifically, federal immigration enforcement policies are progressively delegated to state and local jurisdictions. Two federal initiatives, namely 287(g) and the Secure Communities program, have prompted these enforcement policies. The Illegal Immigration Reform and Immigrant Responsibility Act (IIRIRA) of 1996 created the 287(g) program during the Clinton administration. This enabled state and local law enforcement agencies to partner with immigration agents and allowed 287(g) officers to perform the jobs of immigration enforcement agents. These two programs differ in that Secure Communities does not authorize local enforcement officers to arrest individuals.

Secure Communities existed between 2008 and 2014. This program was designed to identify immigrants in U.S. jails or prisons. If immigrants were stopped by local police officers, arrested, and booked into custody, their fingerprints were subsequently shared with the Federal Bureau of Investigation (FBI) and stored in a database. This allowed ICE access to information on those held in prisons and jails and gave them a technological presence. If the database found that the individual was unlawfully in the U.S., then ICE took over with a goal of deportation.

A 2011 report entitled *Secure Communities by the Numbers: An Analysis of Demographics and Due Process* found that 93 percent of people processed into the database were Latino/a, yet the numbers indicated that Latinos/as comprised 77 percent of the unauthorized population. These numbers are indicative of a program that disproportionately targeted Latino communities. The arrest, detention, and deportation of immigrants heavily relies on profiling—an explicitly racial practice.

In 2014, Secure Communities was replaced by a new program called the Priority Enforcement Program (PEP). While those deported under Secure Communities were overwhelmingly not criminals, PEP focuses on apprehending persons convicted of crimes. However, under PEP, ICE will continue to use detainers. Detainers are written requests used by the Department of Homeland Security, which permit law enforcement agencies to detain individuals beyond their authority. Detention allows ICE to take these individuals into their custody. One of the goals for replacing Secure Communities with PEP was to limit the use of detainers to special circumstances—which include situations when a person has a final order of removal, or if there is satisfactory probable cause that a person is removable. Importantly, detainers have been found to violate the Fourth Amendment right to be secure against unreasonable searches and seizures. Given that these detainers are still being issued, PEP continues many of the same practices that existed under Secure Communities. Further, PEP continues to conflate federal immigration enforcement with local-level policing, which means that racial profiling in enforcement persists.

Race in Birthright Citizenship Policies

"Birthright citizenship" is the legal right to citizenship for all children born in a country's territory, regardless of parentage. Its incorporation into the U.S. Constitution and subsequent legal challenges are intricately connected to race. In 1857, when the Supreme Court ruled that blacks were not U.S. citizens, the nation shifted its attention to birthright citizenship. It was incorporated into the U.S. Constitution under the 14th Amendment, which states that "All persons born or naturalized in the United States, and subject to the jurisdiction thereof, are citizens of the United States and of the state wherein they reside." This amendment guaranteed birthright citizenship for black Americans.

Its application to immigrants' descendants surfaced in the case of Wong Kim Ark, a man born in the U.S. to parents who were Chinese immigrants. Because the Chinese Exclusion Acts prohibited "persons of the Chinese race" from becoming naturalized citizens, Wong Kim Ark's American citizenship was open for interpretation. In 1898, the Supreme Court ruled in favor of Wong Kim Ark. This ruling set legal precedence that children born in the U.S. to undocumented parents have the right to U.S. citizenship.

Race is continually at the center of contemporary debates about birthright citizenship—whether spoken or unspoken. Although undocumented persons vary in their national and ethnic backgrounds, the combination of a shared border and racial discrimination drives xenophobic political interests that spotlight Mexican immigrants and their descendants. Undocumented parents in U.S.-Mexico border states face barriers to obtaining birth certificates for their U.S.-born children. Because officials in some administrative locations refuse to accept the *matrícula consular*, a foreign identification specific to Mexican immigrants, their children are systematically barred from U.S. citizenship.

The 14th Amendment is absent of any racialized language. "All persons" does not specify racial groups. The interpretation and application of the amendment, however, uses race to clarify and exclude certain groups. As such, challenges to the amendment must be examined to ensure equal protection for all persons under the law.

Recommendations and Solutions

The historical relationship between race and immigration underscores the importance of considering how discrimination can persist in today's legal system, even in an era of colorblindness. Race continues to be a factor used to create, interpret, and enforce immigration policies. Extended policing policies are enforced using racial profiling to identify potential undocumented immigrants. Challenges to birthright citizenship target Mexican Americans by excluding the use of foreign identity documents from Mexico. Although the United States is often described as a "nation of immigrants," we must continue to examine which groups remain excluded and why. In light of these questions, we offer the following recommendations and solutions. These recommendations provide information for institutions seeking to eradicate discriminatory policies and practices and guarantee access to human rights for all.

1. *Extended policing.*

- We recommend that federal immigration and local police enforcement agencies discontinue their enforcement collaborations. Although the President's Task Force on 21st Century Policing has previously recommended decoupling federal immigration enforcement from local policing, it has yet to be implemented. Further, we recommend that the Department of Homeland Security end the use of unlawful detainers that continue under the PEP program.
- Identify and eradicate the use of racial profiling as a valid mechanism for denying U.S. documents, for migratory detention, or for the investigation of individuals' and families' documentation status. To this end, law enforcement officers should undergo extensive training and background checks with the goal of identifying racial bias and providing training to reduce negative attitudes. However, racism is beyond the individual as it is embedded in all our social institutions. The consequences of racism are visible in our educational, health care, immigration, and criminal justice inequities. Therefore, it is also critical to hold institutions responsible. This leads us to our next recommendation.
- Increasing data collection can provide a better understanding of the scope and nature of the problem. We recommend systematic data collection on routine stops to see if and where Latinos are

disproportionately profiled. Further, we recommend a database be created where police brutality, abuse, murders, and violence are also documented. *The Guardian*, a British newspaper, has initiated this process. Ultimately, we recommend more transparency across all enforcement levels, including the multifaceted immigration enforcement regime, which includes law enforcement officers, private detention centers, ICE officials, and politicians that create and promote deportation regimes.

2. *Birthright citizenship.*

- To prevent discrimination against immigrants and ethnic minorities, schools, governmental offices, and social service providers should accept foreign forms of identification to allow U.S.-born children access to the rights and privileges associated with American citizenship. Such rights and privileges include access to education and social services.

  o *Education*: Public schools should not inquire about immigration status as part of the enrollment process. If schools must establish that students live within its district, parents can provide a utility bill or lease as a substitute. While it can seem like a race-neutral practice to inquire about immigration status, state variation in the implementation of this practice suggests that it is an attempt to identify and exclude a particular ethnic group.

  o *Social Services*: "Proof of identity" is required to access social services. In some states, however, proof of citizenship is also required. This means that services are inaccessible to American children born to undocumented parents. Because of barriers to obtaining birth certificates, U.S.-born children may never be able to prove citizenship. We recommend that proof of citizenship be removed as a requirement to access social services. This will minimize racially biased practices of screening and detection that disproportionately disadvantage those perceived to be without documentation.

- Create universal programs that provide a social safety net for all U.S. citizens. *Conditional* programs are available only to those who qualify based on a given set of characteristics such as income or employment status. *Universal* programs, by contrast, are available to all citizens. They often receive more public support because it means that taxpayers are contributing to a service that they could also benefit from. Public opinion and funding for social programs is intricately linked to political views on race. The perception that such programs benefit undeserving black and brown families means that while public policy is void of race on its surface, social policies and race can never actually be decoupled. The solution, then, is to provide social services for all U.S. citizens.

- To avoid creating generations of stateless populations, state and federal courts should adopt legal measures to protect birthright citizenship as a key cornerstone of the U.S. Constitution, regardless of parents' documentation status. Further, processes to access documents for children should be non-discriminatory and easy to use, thereby ensuring that all people born within U.S. territory have access to birthright citizenship, regardless of their ethnic background. To ensure that all U.S.-born children have birth certificates, legal and bureaucratic entities should adopt appropriate measures for parents who were previously unable to register their children using foreign identification documents.

- Our final recommendation promotes the eradication of colorblindness as a policy tool. Given that many people believe that we live in a "post-racial" society, we recommend that racism and white supremacy courses be taught with age-appropriate pedagogy as early as elementary school. Rather than reinforcing the idea that one can be blind to race, students should be encouraged to dig deeper into issues of privilege and racial oppression.

Key Resources

Bloemraad, Irene. 2013. "Being American/Becoming American: Birthright Citizenship and Immigrants' Membership in the United States." *Studies in Law, Politics and Society*, 60: 55-84.

Bonilla-Silva, Eduardo. 2003. *Racism Without Racists: Color-blind Racism and the Persistence of Racial Inequality in the United States* Lanham, Md.: Rowman & Littlefield.

Haney-López, I. 1996. *White by law: The Legal Construction of Race*. New York: New York University Press.

Kohli, Aarti, Peter L. Markowitz, and Lisa Chavez. 2011. "Secure Communities by the Numbers: An Analysis of Demographics and Due Process." Berkeley, CA: The Chief Justice Earl Warren Institute on Law and Social Policy.

Menjívar, Cecilia. 2014. "The 'Poli-Migra' Multilayered Legislation, Enforcement Practices, and What We Can Learn About and From Today's Approaches." *American Behavioral Scientist*, 58(13): 1805-1819.

President's Task Force on 21st Century Policing. 2015. *Final Report of the President's Task Force on 21st Century Policing*. Washington, DC: Office of Community Oriented Policing Services

US Department of Homeland Security. 2014. "Immigration Enforcement Actions: 2013." Annual Report, Office of Immigration Statistics, September 2014. Retrieved September 10, 2015. http://www.dhs.gov/sites/default/files/publications/ois_enforcement_ar_2013.pdf

About the Authors

Trenita B. Childers, M.A. is a Ph.D. (expected 2017) candidate in the Sociology department at Duke University, where she earned her master's in Sociology. Her research interests include race/ethnicity, immigration, citizenship, and the social determinants of health. Her dissertation examines the loss of birthright citizenship and mental health among Dominicans of Haitian descent born in the Dominican Republic. Her research has been funded by Duke University, the National Science Foundation, and the U.S. Fulbright Program.

San Juanita García, Ph.D. is a Postdoctoral Fellow in the National Research Service Award Mental Health Services and Systems Research Training Program at the Cecil G. Sheps Center for Health Services Research at the University of North Carolina, Chapel Hill, jointly sponsored by the Department of Psychiatry and Behavioral Sciences at Duke University Medical Center. Her research interests are immigration, race/class/gender, medical sociology, sociology of mental health, and Latina/o sociology. Her research has been funded by the Ford Foundation and the American Sociological Association Minority Fellowship Program (NIMH).

SECTION IV

Criminal (In)Justice

NINE

Gun Violence in the U.S.: Prevalence, Consequences, and Policy Implications

Kellie R. Lynch, Tony P. Love, and Claire M. Renzetti

The Problem

Following mass public shootings in California and Oregon in the spring of 2014, President Obama declared that such incidents were becoming "the norm." To be sure, the number of mass public shootings in the United States has increased significantly since 2011. According to Harvard researchers who compiled statistics for *Mother Jones* magazine, the number of mass public shootings in the U.S. tripled from 2011 to 2014, occurring on average every 64 days; in contrast, from 1982 to 2010, a mass public shooting occurred on average every 200 days. And 2011-2015 marked the period of deadliest mass public shootings in terms of number of people killed and injured, including 20 first graders who were among the 27 people killed during the mass shooting at Sandy Hook Elementary School in Newtown, Connecticut on December 14, 2012. The U.S. leads the world in the number of mass public shootings with 31 percent (90) of the 292 known mass public shootings that took place in 171 countries between 1966 and 2012. Such violent episodes, as horrific as they are, may be the least of our problems when it comes to gun violence, since according to the Centers for Disease Control (CDC), they account for less than 2 percent of total gun deaths in the U.S. each year and less than 1 percent of child gun deaths in this country. Who, then, is most at risk for gun violence perpetration and victimization? And what policy changes may be most effective in reducing gun violence in the U.S.? In this chapter, we review the empirical data that provide answers to these questions.

Research Evidence

It is important to keep in mind that estimates of gun violence may vary depending on how it is defined. For example, the Federal Bureau of Investigation (FBI) has historically defined a mass shooting as an incident in which four or more individuals are killed. In 2013, President Obama lowered the threshold to three or more homicide victims. Nevertheless, such a narrow definition excludes shootings in which fewer than three people are killed, but many are injured. In contrast, Everytown for Gun Safety (www.everytown.org), a social activist group, uses a broad definition that includes incidents in which no one is injured, resulting in a substantially higher number of mass shootings than appears in federal statistics. The Centers for Disease Control and Prevention (CDC)'s National Center for Health Statistics, however, provides annual counts of the number of people killed with guns as well as nonfatal gun injuries. According to the CDC, each year, approximately 32,000 people are killed with guns, but more than half (61 percent) are suicides. An additional 74,000 people are injured in nonfatal gunshot incidents annually. In fact, Americans under the age of 40 are more likely to die from a firearm injury than any specific disease, and women in the U.S. are 11 times more likely to be murdered by a gun than are women in other developed countries.

A widespread belief is that most gun violence is perpetrated by people with serious mental illness, who are perceived by the general public to be "dangerous" and prone to violent behavior. A recent review of the epidemiological research, however, found that while there is an elevated risk of violent behavior among individuals with a serious mental illness, the majority of mentally ill people are never violent. Moreover, these studies show that other population groups—specifically, youth (aged 15-24), males, individuals who are poor and living in economically disadvantaged neighborhoods with high crime rates, and individuals with substance abuse problems—are more likely to perpetrate gun violence, regardless of whether or not they have a mental illness.

Victimization patterns are similar to perpetration patterns. African Americans, males, and individuals between the ages of 18 and 24 are at the highest risk of being killed by a gun in the U.S. In fact, the CDC reports that homicide committed using a firearm is the leading cause of death in the U.S. for non-Hispanic, African Americans between the ages of 15 and 34. State-specific statistics show that rates of gun-related deaths are twice as high for African Americans than whites. Urban areas, particularly with high proportions of racial and ethnic minorities, typically have higher rates of gun death. Young men in urban areas may be at higher risk of being killed by a gun because of the role of guns in drug and/or gang-related crime. In 2008, 92 percent of all gang-related homicides were committed using a gun, which is a 19 percent increase over 1980 gang-related homicides. Further, urban youth are more likely than rural youth to carry guns for protection, intimidation, and to gain respect, putting guns at the center of urban street crime.

There are also important gender differences in both fatal and non-fatal gun violence injury. An analysis by researchers at the federal Bureau of Justice Statistics found that from 1980 to 2008, 82.6 percent of male homicide victims compared to only 17.4 percent of female homicide victims were killed with a firearm. Though males are more likely to be murdered than females (both in general and using a firearm), this same analysis revealed that females were almost six times more likely than males to be murdered by an intimate partner (41.5 percent of females versus 7.1 percent of males). Guns play a crucial role in intimate partner homicide, as intimate partners in the U.S. are more likely to be murdered by a firearm than all other means combined. Further, domestic violence-related gun violence has substantial consequences for the safety of those outside the family. Of mass shootings between 2009 and 2013, 57 percent involved offenders who shot an intimate partner and/or family member.

Although gun-related homicide and crime receive the majority of attention in the media, more people are killed by guns through suicide (6.7 per 100,000 people) than homicide (3.5 per 100,000 people). Rates of homicide and non-fatal gun crime have actually decreased over the past 30 years, but analysis of data from the National Crime Victimization Survey shows that rates of gun-related suicides have declined at much slower rates, even rising in some years. Risk factors for suicides involving guns are also different from those for homicides involving guns. Males, individuals 65 years old and older, and whites have the highest firearm suicide rates in the U.S.

Given the magnitude of firearm-related death and injury in the U.S. each year, gun violence should be considered a public health problem. A 2004 report by the World Health Organization estimated that gun violence in the U.S., including suicide, costs $155 billion each year in expenses related to medical costs and wages lost, with lifetime medical care costing each victim an average of $37,000-$42,000 in 2001 dollars. Similarly, an analysis of physical injuries in the U.S. in 2000 found that firearm-related injuries and fatalities result in the highest lost-productivity costs for men and women in this country.

Though gun violence is a major cause of death and injury for adults, it is also a monumental problem for the nation's children. In an analysis of 24 high-income countries, 87 percent of children aged 14 or younger who were killed by a gun were killed in the U.S. Gun violence impacts children in all areas of the U.S. but in different ways; children in urban areas are more likely to die from gun-related homicide and rural children are more likely to die from accidents or suicides involving guns. In addition to physical injuries, gun violence has serious, negative social and emotional consequences for children and families. Children who have been exposed to gun violence experience a variety of adverse effects, including post-traumatic stress disorder (PTSD), anger or aggression, withdrawal, and desensitization to violence.

Recommendations and Solutions

Whenever the issue of gun violence is discussed, a heated debate over Second Amendment rights is likely to ensue. The Second Amendment to the U.S Constitution reads simply, "A well regulated Militia, being necessary to the security of a free State, the right of the people to keep and bear Arms, shall not be infringed." But this sentence has been interpreted in a variety of ways. For example, one interpretative argument—the states' rights perspective—posits that the amendment offers no guarantees to individuals, but instead protects each state's right to maintain a well-regulated fighting force, thereby allowing wide leeway in terms of the scope of individual gun control legislation. In contrast, the individual rights interpretation, which seems to dominate popular opinion in the U.S., maintains that the Second Amendment guarantees individual citizens the right to gun ownership, thereby rendering any prohibition of firearms unconstitutional.

Although a large segment of the general public currently interprets the Second Amendment as speaking to individual rights, this was not always the case. In fact, in 1939 the Supreme Court ruled in *U.S. v. Miller* that the constitutional right guaranteed by the Second Amendment relates only to a state's well-regulated militia and not to an individual citizen's right to bear arms. Moreover, from 1959 to 1966, Gallup polls showed that when asked, "Do you think there should be a law that would ban the possession of handguns, except by the police and other authorized persons?" more Americans replied yes than no. From 1967 on, however, the numbers have been reversed and the gap has widened each year. In 2015, 27 percent of respondents to this same question replied that they supported a law banning the possession of handguns, while 72 percent opposed such a law. Nevertheless, while most Americans polled do not favor banning guns, they do favor stricter gun control laws. In 2015 Gallup polling, 15 percent of Americans polled who said they were dissatisfied with the nation's laws and policies on guns felt that the laws and policies were too strict, whereas 38 percent who were dissatisfied said that the laws and policies were not strict enough.

In 2008 the Supreme Court once again weighed in, ruling in a 5-4 decision in *District of Columbia v. Heller* that the Second Amendment guarantees the right of individuals to maintain a firearm in their home for self-defense. The Court, however, also stated that the Second Amendment does not promise a "right to keep and carry any weapon whatsoever in any manner whatsoever and for whatever purpose." In doing so, the Court clearly indicated that the Second Amendment does not prohibit gun control laws and policies that limit who may possess firearms, what kinds of firearms they may possess, or where they may possess them.

One particularly promising approach to gun control and the goal of reducing gun violence is the public health model. In 2015, eight health professional organizations (American Academy of Family Physicians, American Academy of Pediatrics, American College of Emergency Physicians, American Congress of Obstetricians and Gynecologists, American College of Physicians, American College of Surgeons, American Psychiatric Association, and American Public Health Association) along with the American Bar Association publicly issued their stand to reduce gun violence in the United States and voiced their support for a public health approach to the problem. This model conceptualizes gun injuries and deaths as a major public health problem that should be addressed the way other public health problems are addressed. For example, this approach proposes the use of advertising, similar to smoking cessation campaigns, that seeks to convey the message to the general public that the easy availability and misuse of firearms may have deleterious effects on people's health.

Additionally, public health approaches to gun violence acknowledge the role of mental illness in gun violence generally and suicide specifically, and do not violate the Second Amendment. Studies show that increased restrictions on firearms create a significant decrease in suicide rates. Given this information and other links between mental health and mass shootings, proponents of the public health perspective on gun violence advocate increased access to mental health care, but do not advocate that all persons with mental health issues be lumped into the same category of prohibition.

Specific policy recommendations from the public health model include: universal background checks of gun purchasers, elimination of physician "gag laws," restrictions on the manufacture and sale of military-style assault weapons and large-capacity magazines for civilian use, and research to support strategies for reducing firearm-related injuries and deaths.

1. Universal background checks.

President Barack Obama issued at least 25 executive orders on gun ownership. In response to health organizations' call for more stringent and comprehensive background checks, one executive order tightened the background check system by broadening the scope of who is considered a firearms dealer, ensuring that states improve their background check reporting and collaborate to close blind spots, allocating resources to make the background check system more efficient, and requiring background checks for every purchaser regardless of where the firearms purchase occurs. Additional criteria include increased availability of mental health treatment and reporting of relevant mental health characteristics to the background check system. But calls for more stringent background checks have been made in the wake of virtually every mass shooting since Columbine in 1999, and very few of these have translated into actual legislation. Bipartisan support is necessary for such bills to pass, and that support has been elusive. Once on the books, though, law enforcement agencies must have the resources to aggressively enforce the laws.

2. Eliminate gag laws.

Physician "gag laws" refer to legislation that prohibits physicians from talking to their patients about certain topics. Currently, it is illegal in many states for physicians to speak to their patients about the possible negative health outcomes of firearm ownership. Most of these state laws allow patients to refuse to answer questions concerning firearm ownership and safety. Some include language that prohibits physicians or other medical personnel from inquiring about gun ownership and storage and from discriminating against gun owners (e.g., refusing to care for a patient who owns guns or who will not disclose information about gun ownership and safety), and prohibits harassment of a patient about firearm ownership. Violations of the laws may lead to sanctions from the state Board of Medicine including suspension, loss of license, and a fine up to $10,000. Physicians, of course, should not refuse care to a patient because he or she owns a gun, and they shouldn't "harass" patients about owning guns. But physicians are perhaps in the best position to determine whether a patient could pose a risk of injury to themselves or others if given access to a firearm. Gag laws should be rescinded or revised to allow physicians the liberty to discuss possible proactive, protective strategies for promoting firearm safety.

3. Restrict the manufacture and sale of certain firearms and ammunition.

The eight health professional organizations cited above and the American Bar Association agree, as do we, that there is a need for restrictions on military-style weapons and high-capacity magazines because the widespread availability of these weapons represents "a grave danger to the public." This position is based on the common sense idea that decreasing the number of firearms explicitly designed to increase killing capacity should decrease the likelihood of casualties resulting from mass shootings.

4. Commitment to research.

The public health response to gun violence includes a call for increased research on the problem. Epidemiologists often shift their focus, and their research funds, toward an emerging public health problem, and given the scope of gun violence in the U.S., the public health model posits that a commitment to research on gun violence in this country is warranted. But gun violence research has been substantially hampered by what has amounted to a ban on such research by the federal government. In the 1997 Appropriations Bill, Congress stipulated that none of the funds made available to the Centers for Disease Control and Prevention for injury prevention and control research could be used to advocate or promote gun control. In 2012, this restriction was expanded to include all Health and Human Services agencies. It was not until after the mass shooting in Sandy Hook, Connecticut, that President Obama sought to overturn this ban, but by then, many researchers had turned their attention to other issues. Currently, the

National Institutes of Health (NIH) has several funding mechanisms for research on the health determinants and consequences of violence and its prevention, especially gun violence. Hopefully, this funding will generate rigorous empirical research to both identify and fill knowledge gaps with regard to gun violence and its prevention.

In summary, gun violence is a serious, yet preventable public health problem in the U.S. that destroys thousands of lives and costs the U.S. economy billions of dollars annually. There have been increased efforts in recent years to reduce and prevent gun violence by introducing policies that do not infringe upon the constitutional rights of Americans, but save lives and reduce injuries and their consequences. Despite the complexities of addressing gun violence in the U.S., it is critical for researchers, politicians, and other professionals to continuously implement and evaluate efforts that reduce the unnecessary damage resulting from the widespread and largely unfettered availability of firearms in this country.

Key Resources

Andres, Antonio Rodriguez and Katherine Hempstead. 2011. "Gun Control and Suicide: The Impact of State Firearms Regulations in the United States, 1995-2004." *Health Policy*, 101:95-103.

Centers for Disease Control and Prevention (CDC). 2015. *Web-based Injury Statistics Query and Reporting System (WISQARS)*. Atlanta, GA: National Center for Injury Prevention and Control. http://www.cdc.gov/injury/wisqars/fatal.html

Cooke, Brian K., Emily R. Goddard, Almari Ginory, Jason A. Demery, and Tonia L Werner. 2012. "Firearms Inquiries in Florida: 'Medical Privacy' or Medical Neglect?" *Journal of the American Academy of Psychiatry Law*, 40:399-408.

Corso, Phaedra S., James A. Mercy, Thomas R. Simon, Eric A. Finkelstein, and Ted R. Miller. 2007. "Medical Costs and Productivity Losses Due to Interpersonal and Self-directed Violence in the United States." *American Journal of Preventive Medicine*, 32:474-482.

David Hemenway, Tomoko Shinoda-Tagawa, and Matthew Miller. 2002. "Firearm Availability and Female Homicide Victimization Rates among 25 Populous High-income Countries." *Journal of American Medical Women's Association*, 57:100-104.

Kalesan, Binder, Sowmya Vasan, Matthew E. Mobily, Marcos D. Villarreal, Patrick Hlavacek, Sheldon Teperman, Jeffrey A. Fagan, and Sandro Galea. 2014. "State-specific, Racial and Ethnic Heterogeneity in Trends of Firearm-related Fatality Rates in the USA from 2000 to 2010". *BMJ open*, doi:10.1136/bmjopen-2014-005628.

Lankford, Adam. 2016. "Are America's Public Mass Shooters Unique? A Comparative Analysis of Offenders in the United States and Other Countries." *International Journal of Comparative and Applied Criminal Justice*, 40(2):171-183.

Nance, M. L., B. G. Carr, M. J. Kallan, C. C. Branas and D. J. Wiebe. 2010. Variation in Pediatric and Adolescent Firearm Mortality Rates in Rural and Urban US Counties. *Pediatrics*, 125:1112-1118.

Schildkraut, Jaclyn and Tiffany Cox Hernandez. 2014. "Laws that Bit the Bullet: A Review of Legislative Responses to School Shootings." *American Journal of Criminal Justice*, 39(2):358-374.

Swanson, Jeffrey W., E. Elizabeth McGinty, Seena Fazel, S., and Vickie M. Mays. 2015. "Mental Illness and Reduction of Gun Violence and Suicide: Bringing Epidemiologic Research to Policy." *Annals of Epidemiology*, 25:366-376.

Waters, H., Hyder, A., Rajkotia, Y., Basu, S., Rehwinkel, J.A., and Butchart, A. 2004. "The economic dimensions of interpersonal violence. Department of Injuries and Violence Prevention." Geneva: World Health Organization. http://whqlibdoc.who.int/publications/2004/9241591609.pdf?ua=1

Webster, Daniel W. and Jon S. Vernick. (Eds.) 2013. *Reducing Gun Violence in America: Informing Policy with Evidence and Analysis.* Baltimore, MD: Johns Hopkins University Press.

Weinberger, Steven E., David B. Hoyt, Hal C. Lawrence, Saul Levin, Douglas E. Henley, Errol R. Alden, Dean Wilkinson, George C. Benjamin, and William C. Hubbard. 2015. "Firearms-related Injury and Death in the United States: A Call to Action from 8 Health Professional Organizations and the American Bar Association". *Annals of Internal Medicine*, 162:513-516.

About the Authors

Kellie R. Lynch, Ph.D. will be joining the Department of Criminal Justice at the University of Texas at San Antonio as an Assistant Professor in August 2016. She completed her doctoral training in the Department of Psychology at the University of Kentucky, and worked as a graduate student researcher at the University of Kentucky's Center for Research on Violence Against Women and Center on Drug and Alcohol Research. Her research interests include intimate partner violence, implementation of gun-related policy, and psychosocial theories related to sexual assault and victim blaming.

Tony P. Love, Ph.D. is an Assistant Professor in the Sociology Department at the University of Kentucky. His areas of interest include criminology, deviant behavior, and social psychology, and he specializes in experimental research methods. His most recent research focuses on inequitable outcomes in the juvenile justice system. He has co-authored articles in the *American Sociological Review*, *Deviant Behavior*, *Sociological Perspectives*, and *Violence Against Women*.

Claire M. Renzetti, Ph.D. is the Judi Conway Patton Endowed Chair in the Center for Research on Violence Against Women, and Professor and Chair of the Sociology Department at the University of Kentucky. She is editor of the international, interdisciplinary journal *Violence Against Women*, co-editor with Jeffrey Edleson of the Interpersonal Violence book series for Oxford University Press, and editor of the Gender and Justice book series for University of California Press. She has authored or edited 21 books as well as numerous book chapters and articles in professional journals. She has held elected and appointed positions on the governing bodies of several national professional organizations, including President of the Society for the Study of Social Problems (2006).

TEN

American Prisons: Consequences of Mass Incarceration

Alana Van Gundy

The Problem

The United States incarcerates approximately 2.3 million individuals, making it the nation with the leading incarceration rate. Over the last 40 years, the American prison population has increased by 500 percent, with the highest rates per capita in Louisiana, Oklahoma, Alabama, Arkansas, and Mississippi. Primarily a result of the War on Drugs, mandatory sentencing policies, and the Three Strikes Laws, this increase includes a higher proportion of females, special needs individuals, elderly offenders, nonviolent drug offenders, and those that are incarcerated for life without parole, adding to the increasing financial burden of the system of corrections. In 1980, for example, close to 41,000 people were imprisoned for nonviolent drug-related offenses and by 2014 almost 500,000 individuals were incarcerated for nonviolent drug-related offenses. While the United States houses only 5 percent of the world's population, its prisons are home to more than 25 percent of the world's incarcerated population, leaving it the clear leader for incarceration efforts.

Close to 12 million individuals revolve in and out of American jails in one year, with an average of 731,000 people being housed in jail facilities daily. According to a 2015 Vera Institute of Justice report, American jails were intended to house the dangerous, the individuals at risk for fleeing, yet they have become what the Vera Institute of Justice called "massive warehouses primarily for those too poor to post even low bail or too sick for existing community resources to manage." Up to 75 percent of the jail population is detained for non-violent property, traffic, or public order offenses.

This churning of individuals in and out of incarceration facilities results in dangerous levels of overcrowding, issues with disease control, increasing suicide rates in prisons and jails, and multiple human rights violations. Additional impacts of mass incarceration include severed family relationships; lack of job opportunities and felon disenfranchisement; disparate impacts on racial and ethnic minorities; loss of public benefits; and educational, social, and severe economic and emotional consequences for children of incarcerated parents.

Research Evidence

Mass incarceration is a significant public health and public safety issue, for society and for individuals during and post-incarceration. A nation that incarcerates individuals instead of offering primary prevention programs or appropriately implemented rehabilitation programs is prone to multiple issues with economic and social oppression, high financial costs, and dangerous environments for those that are incarcerated.

Issues with Overcrowding, Disease Control, and Suicides

- Prisons in the United States are almost all above capacity; some are at capacities as high as 173 percent. While most prisons are adult male facilities, juvenile facilities and female facilities are also at high levels of over-capacity.
- The Federal Bureau of Prisons has been forced to place two or three bunks in a cell and convert open bays and television rooms into mass sleeping quarters to meet housing needs. This has resulted in large open rooms that do not allow for those that are incarcerated to be properly classified and housed.
- Prison overcrowding threatens public safety and state budgets, and a 2006 study conducted by the State of Washington showed that while incarcerating violent offenders serves to protect public safety, the increased use of imprisonment for nonviolent offenders leads to negative returns.
- The massive amounts of overcrowding and the closeness of quarters have made infection and diseases difficult, if not impossible to control. The spread of infectious diseases includes HIV/AIDS, sexually transmitted diseases, Hepatitis B and C, tuberculosis, valley fever, and Legionnaire's disease.
- In prisons, suicides kill more incarcerated individuals than accidents, homicide, and drug overdoses combined. Of all deaths in state and

federal prisons in 2011, 5.5 percent were due to suicide. Research has linked the prevalence of suicide to the issue of overcrowding and the use of solitary confinement.

Human Rights Violations

The United Nations Standard Minimum Rules for the Treatment of Prisoners and the Bangkok Rules govern the treatment of female offenders and offer a framework by which to measure the prevalence of human rights violations in jails and prisons.

- Overcrowding is viewed as a human rights violation according to these human rights governance doctrines. Additionally, the large open rooms housing those that are incarcerated violate the requirement that each prisoner shall occupy by night a cell or room by her/himself unless there is a "temporary crowding" issue.
- In an era of mass incarceration, inmates can wait months for a standard doctor's visit (if they are even able to be seen). They are often provided substandard medical care, and some may not be able to afford visits, medication, or time away from their prison employment. As a ward of the state or federal government, those that are incarcerated must be provided for at a "basic minimal level standard of care," and not doing so constitutes a human rights violation.
- Female offenders are often the victims of medical and health care violations as prisons shackle women that are in labor and delivery and do not house an ob-gyn physician on staff or provide gender-specific toiletries. Additionally, they are prone to heart disease, breast and ovarian cancer, and co-occurring mental health disorders at higher rates than males, so not providing doctors that are familiar with or specialize in gender-centric health care is of specific harm to them.
- The U.N. doctrines also discuss that incarcerated individuals must not be placed in restraints as punishment; each person requires daily visits by doctors and an immediate doctor visit upon entrance into custody; and all individuals that are incarcerated must be afforded books, education, and appropriate programming. In an era of mass incarceration, the sheer numbers make this an impossibility, leaving the prisons again as perpetrators of human rights violations.

Collateral Damage to Families and Children

- 2.7 million children in the United States have an incarcerated parent. It has been estimated that over 4 million children have a parent that is under community supervision. This equates to almost 4 percent of all American children that have lost a parent to incarceration (almost 7 percent watch their parent complete community supervision) and as a result, their lives will be impacted by that social stigma, the loss of income and economic stability, and the emotional issues that are related to the loss of a parent. Additionally, children of incarcerated parents are at higher risk of becoming incarcerated themselves.
- 87 percent of all females that are incarcerated are mothers, and the majority of them were single parents with sole custody or the breadwinner of the home. Maternal incarceration often results in the child being placed into foster care. Females that are incarcerated are also placed in facilities that are much farther away from their families than male inmates so these children are often unable to visit their mothers throughout their incarceration.
- Children often have short-term effects such as nightmares and flashbacks of their parents being arrested and long-term effects such as lack of attachment to others; severe emotional and behavioral problems; high levels of anxiety, depression, withdrawal, shame, guilt, or hypervigilance; internalizing behaviors such as eating disorders and cutting; and externalizing behaviors such as anger, aggression, and hostility towards others.
- Children of incarcerated parents often have school-related problems, peer relationship problems, poor academic performance, fear of attending school, and higher suspension and dropout rates than children who do not have an incarcerated parent.
- When a family member is incarcerated, it negatively impacts economic and social standing, physical and mental health, employment and earnings, family attachments and social support systems, and perceptions of the police, courts, and criminal justice system.

Obstacles to Re-entry

- Individuals that are incarcerated must adapt into the subculture of the prison in order to be able to survive the environment. This results in them having significant obstacles to overcome upon re-entry, re-learning a pro-social value system upon release, and trying to rebuild their lives with conditional limitations on their lives and restrictions on their access to resources.

- After being released from incarceration facilities, individuals are impacted by significant barriers. They lose to the right to vote in many states, hold public office, earn specific certifications (nursing and medical for example), gain public or housing assistance, hold an unrestricted driver's license, and to become foster or adoptive parents. Often they are unable to regain custody of their own children.
- Released individuals rely heavily on their families for housing, employment, and support post-incarceration. If they do not have a strong, pro-social family support system, successful re-entry is much more difficult.
- Released prisoners have a difficult time finding employment in the year after re-entry. Employment is often considered the primary factor in successful reintegration.
- While medical care is not of high caliber within institutional facilities, those that are incarcerated are often able to gain access to medication to control diseases, and chronic and infectious conditions, and medications for mental illness. After release, they are often unable to continue health care programming due to geographical or financial limitations.
- Upon release, offenders must abide by stringent parole conditions. These conditions often limit their access to jobs, send them back into the same community in which they originally engaged in their criminal behavior, and place conditional employment and housing restrictions that often cannot be overcome.

Racial and Ethnic Disparities

- African Americans are incarcerated at six times the rate of whites.
- While African Americans and Hispanic Americans comprise around 25 percent of the American population, they are 58 percent of the prison population.
- Five times as many whites report using illicit drugs but African Americans are incarcerated for drug offenses at ten times the rate of whites.

- African American males between the ages of 30 and 34 have the highest incarceration rate of any other combination of race, gender, and age.
- In 2010, African American women were incarcerated at three times the rate of white women.
- Incarceration of minorities at a high rate disproportionately impacts women of color and their children. The incarceration of a parent is a significant risk factor, leaving children of minority parents at increased risk of becoming offenders.
- In totality, African Americans and Hispanic Americans are the most disenfranchised population pre-, during, and post-incarceration.

Recommendations and Solutions

The following actions are critical to addressing the consequences of mass incarceration and decreasing the U.S. reliance on incarceration as a punishment:

1. Revisit the salience of policies such as the War on Drugs and Three Strikes Laws.

The War on Drugs, mandatory sentencing, and the Three Strikes Laws have disproportionately affected those that are socially, economically, and politically oppressed. These forms of legislation have been responsible for a large jump in prison incarceration, impacting individuals, families, and society.

2. Increase the focus on alternatives to incarceration.

Consequences of incarceration are tremendous at multiple levels. Diverting non-serious offenders or offenders that are not at risk for reoffending is critical for the long-term public health and safety issues for the individuals and the children of the individuals. Maintaining the family as a unit by the use of community corrections can increase social bonds and attachment of the parent and provide an insulating factor for the child.

3. Address criminological risk predictors by offering government programs and assistance.

These include primary and secondary educational and vocational training, social assistance (including the removal of disenfranchisement laws and obstacles to public assistance), and restorative justice-based victimization programs.

4. Quantify the social and economic impact of incarceration on re-entry/restoration of society/cost to taxpayers.

The cost of criminal justice and the system of corrections is commonly the number one government expenditure. Educating the general public on the financial cost of incarceration, the social cost, and familial consequences must be quantified so that taxpayers are aware of the significant financial impact of mass imprisonment. This education must include a cost comparison table for primary preventative programming, alternatives to incarceration, and incarceration. Additionally, future cost analysis should be included.

5. Begin a new social movement, akin to the civil rights movement.

In order to effectively combat the detrimental effects of mass incarceration, a new social movement must occur. Instead of being a "prisoner's movement," this movement must include those that are incarcerated, individuals in the general public, educators in the academy, and government officials. It must focus on the intersection between race and crime, social oppression, disproportionate sentencing, felon disenfranchisement, and barriers to successful re-entry. It must ultimately advance crime- and victim-related programming, continued medical treatment and disease control, and reduce the long-term individual, economic, and social effect of incarceration.

Key Resources

Alexander, Michelle. 2010. *The New Jim Crow: Mass Incarceration in the Age of Colorblindness.* New York, NY: The New Press.

Blackmon, Douglas A. 2009. *Slavery by another Name: The Re-enslavement of Black Americans from the Civil War to World War II.* New York, NY: Anchor Publishing.

Clear, Todd and James Austin. 2009. "Reducing Mass Incarceration: Implications of the Iron Law of Prison Populations." *Harvard Law and Policy Review,* 3:307-327.

Foster, Holly and John Hagan. 2009. "The Mass Incarceration of Parents in America: Issues of Race/Ethnicity, Collateral Damage to Children, and Prisoner Reentry." *The Annals of the American Academy of Political and Social Science,* 623:179-194.

Gottschalk, Marie. 2006. *The Prison and the Gallows: The Politics of Mass Incarceration in America.* Cambridge, UK: Cambridge University Press.

About The Author

Alana Van Gundy, Ph.D. is an Associate Professor of Justice and Community Studies at Miami University, where she is also the Coordinator of the Criminal Justice Program. Her research focuses on testing gender-based delinquency models on females to identify gender-specific risk predictor variables, programming efforts for incarcerated women, and the intersectionality between race and gender.

SECTION V

Looking Forward

ELEVEN

The Surprising Link between Sustainability and Social Justice

Amitai Etzioni

L arge segments of the world experienced a major financial shakeup in 2008, followed by a major economic downturn in the United States and Europe, especially in southern Europe and Ireland. Unemployment has remained high, especially among the young, and many millions of people lost not merely their jobs, but also their homes, their investments, and their pension funds, with many more having to settle for low-paying jobs providing little to no benefits. While emerging economies—China included—initially held up much better, they too experienced a significant slowdown in economic growth rates. This economic downturn (and rising inequality) has contributed to the rise of political alienation; the rise of a variety of right-wing expressions including xenophobia, racism, and anti-Semitism; and support for radical right-wing parties and politicians. What do these developments portend for the future?

One possibility is that economic development will return to a high growth pathway. As a result, what might be called the "legitimacy of affluence" will be restored. The overwhelming majority of people will again be content with their condition, their society, and their polity. However, a considerable number of scholars hold that it may prove impossible to return to a high growth economy able to provide sufficient employment opportunities, due to increased automation and a greater extraction of labor from fewer workers. Others cite sustainability issues, believing that we face a world in which high growth rates (and, hence, affluence) cannot serve as the source of human contentment, due to environmental conditions, as well as social tensions resulting from growing inequality and rising demands. From the perspective of the affluent society, if the future unfolds in one of these less favorable ways, one must wonder if we shall bear witness to the continued rise in prominence of right-wing fringe groups (e.g., The Golden Dawn, English Defence League, Geert Wilders' Freedom Party, the Jobbik party, and an increasingly radical Tea Party). Or, can one identify other sources of contentment for those who, while having achieved an income level that enables them to meet their "basic" needs, will live in a more austere, less growth-centered, environment? What other sources of legitimacy can be developed that are not based on a continually rising standard of living?

I see great merit in shifting the focus of our actions from seeking ever-greater wealth to investing more of our time and resources in social lives, public action, and spiritual and intellectual activities—on communitarian pursuits. In small ways, this transformation is already underway. For example, a growing number of people choose to work less and to spend more time with their children. Such a society has a much smaller ecological footprint than the affluence-chasing society and hence helps cope with the triple challenge: the deteriorating environment, smart machines killing many jobs while generating few, and rising discontent.

The main merits of this society though lie elsewhere. The preponderance of the relevant evidence shows that as societies grow more affluent, the contentment of their members does not much increase. For example, between 1962 and 1987, the Japanese per capita income more than tripled, yet Japan's overall happiness remained constant over that period. Similarly, in 1970, the average American income could buy over 60 percent more than it could in the 1940s, yet average happiness did not increase. Gaining a good life through ever-higher levels of consumption is a Sisyphean activity. Only finding new sources of meaning in life can bring higher levels of contentment.

While at first blush such a major cultural shift is hard to imagine, one needs to recall that for most of history, work and commerce were not valorized; instead, devotion, learning, chivalry, and being involved in public affairs were. True, these were often historically only accessible to a sliver of the population, while the poor were shut out from such things and forced to work for those who led the chosen life. However, capping consumption would now make it possible for all the population to lead a less active economic life and a more active social, communal, and spiritual—i.e. communitarian—life.

Abraham Maslow pointed out that humans have a hierarchy of needs. At the bottom are basic human necessities; once these are sated, affection and self-esteem are next in line, leading finally to "self-actualization." It follows that as long as the acquisition and consumption of goods satisfy basic creature comforts—safety, shelter, food, clothing, health care, and education—expanding the reach of those goods contributes to genuine human contentment. However, once consumption is used to satisfy Maslow's higher needs, it turns into consumerism—and consumerism becomes a social disease. Indeed, more and more consumption in affluent societies serves artificial needs manufactured by those who market the products in question. For instance, first women and then men were taught that they smelled bad and needed to purchase deodorants. Men, who used to wear white shirts and grey flannel suits, learned that they "had to" purchase a variety of shirts and suits, and that last year's clothing was not proper in the year that followed. Soon, it was not just suits but also cars, ties, handbags, sunglasses, watches, and numerous other products that had to be constantly replaced to keep up with the latest trends.

The new post-affluence society would liberate people from these obsessions and encourage them to fulfill their higher needs once their basic needs have been satisfied. None of this entails dropping wholly out of the economic or technological world. The shift to a less consumerist society and a more communitarian one should not be used to call on the poor to enjoy their misery; everyone is entitled to a secure provision of their basic needs. Instead, those who have already "made it" would cap their focus on their economic activities.

A society that combines capping consumption and work with dedication to communitarian pursuits would obviously be much less taxing on the environment, material resources, and the climate, than consumerism and the level of work that paying for it requires. Social activities (such as spending more time with one's children) require time and personal energy, but do not mandate large material or financial outlays. The same holds true for cultural and spiritual activities such as prayer, meditation, enjoying and making music and art, playing sports, and adult education. Playing chess with plastic pieces is as enjoyable as playing it with mahogany pieces. Reading Shakespeare in a paper-bound edition made of recycled paper is as enlightening as reading his work in a leather-bound edition. And the Lord does not listen more to prayers from those who wear expensive garments than from those who wear a sack.

Less obvious are the ways a socially active society is more likely to advance social justice than the affluent society. Social justice, in part, entails transferring wealth from those disproportionately endowed to those who are underprivileged. A major reason such reallocation of wealth has been very limited in affluent societies is that those who command the "extra" assets tend also to be those who are politically powerful. Promoting social justice by organizing those with less and forcing those in power to yield has had limited success in democratic countries and led to massive bloodshed in others. However, if those in power embrace the capped culture and economy, they will have little reason to refuse to share their "surplus." This thesis is supported by the behavior of middle class people who are committed to the values of giving and attending to the least among us—values prescribed by many religions and by left liberalism.

Key Resources

Easterlin, Richard. 1973. "Does Money Buy Happiness?" *The Public Interest*, 30:3-10.

Etzioni, Amitai. 2013. "A Silk Purse out of a Sow's Ear." *Journal of Modern Wisdom*, 2:40-49.

Gordon, Robert J. 2016. *The Rise and Fall of American Growth: The U.S. Standard of Living since the Civil War.* Princeton, NJ: Princeton University Press.

Maslow, Abraham H. 1943. "A Theory of Human Motivation" *Psychological Review*, 50(4):370–396.

Soergel, Andrew. 2015. "Unemployment Indicators Only Tell Part of the Story." *U.S. News & World Report*, (June 19). http://www.usnews.com/news/articles/2015/06/19/the-problem-with-the-labor-departments-unemployment-indicators

About the Author

Amitai Etzioni, Ph.D. is University Professor and Professor of International Affairs, and Director of the Institute for Communitarian Policy Studies at George Washington University. He is author of numerous books, with his latest, *Privacy in a Cyber Age*, published last year by Palgrave MacMillan. He has been a guest scholar at the Brookings Institution and served as a Senior Advisor to the White House during the Carter Administration. He was named among the top 100 American intellectuals as measured by academic citations in Richard Posner's book, *Public Intellectuals: A Study of Decline*, and he has been frequently interviewed by media outlets.

TWELVE

Techno-fallacies in the Search for Solutions to Social Problems

Gary T. Marx

Many [technical means] are excellent when kept in their places, but when pushed forward as infallible methods, they become forms of quackery.

Dashiell Hammett

In recent decades I have been studying efforts to hard-engineer solutions to soft-social problems, particularly as this involves culture and questions of law, order, security, and surveillance. I sought to understand the ideas associated with efforts to solve problems through science and technology. What I learned about the importance of analyzing the culture of social problem solutions for law and order questions applies to other issues.

In contrast to the previous articles in this volume, which focus directly on problems such as the environment, health, poverty, discrimination, and violence, this chapter argues that how we think about problems, in particular the search for quick technical solutions, can also be a problem. It is a problem in failing to see how the parts of the social order are interdependent (they are "systemic") and interventions into complex, complicated, and fluid social situations will rarely make a problem disappear. Even when there is overall improvement, there will often be unwanted surprises—whether in some ways worsening the situation or bringing new problems.

Among the nations of the world, the United States most clearly reflects the optimistic, techno-surveillance worldview found within a broader technocratic and commercial celebratory ethos. Statements about technical solutions to social problems, whether made by those technocrats, government officials, aspiring politicians, merchants, or interest groups, need to be analyzed for their empirical, logical, and value components.

In 1928 Lyndon Johnson, in his first job interview to be a teacher, was asked where he stood on the then-contentious issue of Darwin and evolution. Knowing there were differences of opinion, he paused before saying he thought he could teach it either way. So it is with many of the great debates about social problems. Without careful analysis persons of good will (and not so good will) can take strongly opposed positions on a given social issue without necessarily being fools, liars or compassionless. Rather, as with the tale of the blind persons and the pachyderm, they are focused on different parts of the elephant.

The difficulty of agreeing on what concepts mean and on how best to measure and assess a problem are factors here, as are multiple, competing and often unclear goals. In the search for solutions, strongly held views can result in a narrowing of vision associated with rhetorical omissions, exaggerations, intellectual short circuiting, the failure to consider costs, along with presumed benefits, and the long as well as the short run. Sometimes the costs of action can be greater than of inaction.

Some of Lyndon Johnson's indecision regarding the most contentious issue of 1928 applies today. While not full Greek tragedies in which a virtue is also a flaw, the multiple goals and complications of a dynamic empirical world offer a vast tableau for disagreement and can result in unwanted consequences and partial victories (if that). Interested parties must remain aware, weigh (if not necessarily balance) what is at stake, tolerate second- and third-best outcomes, and try to identify and then mitigate unwanted collateral consequences.

The empirical record itself often does not clearly and strongly point in one direction. Even with eyes wide open, goodwill, competent agents, and best practices, the actions taken (or not taken) with respect to a social problem may have multiple consequences for legitimate values and interests—serving some while undermining others and almost always involving trade-offs. No amount of research, training, new tools, policy analysis, or public relations can alter that. We can't have it all; repasts always cost someone something, somewhere, sometime.

The bountiful optimism of the Renaissance, the Enlightenment, and utilitarianism meet their match in the natural and social complexity, fluidity, contradictions, and limitations of the world. We are rarely prescient or adequately prepared for the full consequences of innovation and social change.

Avoid Techno-Fallacies and Ask About Ethics

The worldviews of those concerned with social issues such as those discussed in this book involve problem definitions, explanations, justifications, and directions for action. They contain basic assumptions about the social world, varying degrees of certainty about its truths, and an intermingling of values and facts. It is important to approach statements made about social problems in a critical fashion—whether we initially agree or disagree with the ideas. Toward that end, I next identify some fallacies often seen in discussions of social problems, particularly as this involves using technology as the basis of a solution. I conclude with some questions that can help surface the ethical implications of efforts to deal with social problems.

In listening to discussions of social problems over several decades I often heard things that, given my knowledge and values, sounded wrong, much as a musician hears off-key notes. The off-key notes can involve elements of substance as well as styles of mind and ways of reasoning. I have identified a number of "information age techno-fallacies." Sometimes these fallacies are frontal and direct; more often they are tacit—buried within seemingly commonsense, unremarkable assertions. The emphasis here is on showing how some aspects of this worldview are empirically wrong, logically inconsistent, and morally questionable.

Beliefs may be fallacious in different ways. Some are empirically false or illogical. With appropriate evidence and argument, persons of goodwill holding diverse political perspectives and values may be able to see how they are fallacious, or in need of qualification. Fallacies may also involve normative statements about what matters and is desirable, and beliefs about causes and responsibility. These reflect disagreements about scientific explanation and values and value priorities. To label a normative belief a fallacy more clearly reflects the point of view of the labeler. However, normative positions are often informed by empirical assumptions (e.g., favoring rewards over punishments because the latter is seen to be more effective or blaming the social order rather than the individual). In sniffing out fallacies, one must identify and evaluate the intermingling of fact and value and the quality of the facts.

At a very general level, people often agree on what values are most important (though they often dissent over prioritizing and implementing these). Disagreements also commonly occur over what evaluation measure(s) and specific tools for judgment are most appropriate and over how evidence is to be interpreted—both with respect to what it says empirically and to its meaning for a given value.

My approach to analyzing the rhetoric of technology advocacy follows in the broad tradition of scholars such as Mumford, Ellul, Postman, and Mander. While there are fallacies (as well as truths) unique to particular problems or tools, the emphasis here is on ideas that apply across these. Among five types of fallacy, the most important for social problems are:

I.   Fallacies of Technological Determinism and Neutrality

    A. The Fallacy of Autonomous Technology and Emanative Development and Use (the belief that there is an inner logic of development and once a tool appears it can't be stopped)

    B. The Fallacy of Neutrality (the idea that technology is necessarily more objective than humans and the failure to see that someone has had the resources and will to develop technology in a particular way)

    C. The Fallacy of Quantification (the notion that things are only real if they can be counted)

    D. The Fallacy That the Facts Speak for Themselves (facts are "socially constructed" from the rich flow of reality as some aspects are singled out and others ignored)

II. Fallacies of Scientific and Technical Perfection

    A. The Fallacy of the 100 Percent Fail-Safe System (face it, stuff happens!)

    B. The Fallacy of the Sure Shot (the assumption of precision)

    C. The Fallacy of Delegating Decision-Making Authority to the Machine (this is a cop-out in which those who develop and apply the machines avoid moral responsibility)

    D. The Fallacy of the Free Lunch or Painless Dentistry (the idea that solutions come without costs

    E. The Fallacy That the Means Should Determine the Ends (here, instead of saying how can we best meet our goal, the question becomes how can we use this tool)

    F. The Fallacy That Technology Will Always Remain the Solution Rather Than Become the Problem (the tools that contribute to global warming)

III. Fallacies Involving Subjects

    A. The Fallacy That Individuals Are Best Controlled through Fear

B. The Fallacy of a Passive, Non-Reactive Environment (failure to see the systemic aspects and that subjects act back in pursuing their interests)

C. The Fallacy of Implied Consent and Free Choice (manipulating subjects by making them an offer they can't refuse)

D. The Fallacy That If Critics Question the Means, They Must Necessarily Be Indifferent or Opposed to the Ends

E. The Fallacy That Only the Guilty Have to Fear the Development of Intrusive Technology (or If You Have Done Nothing Wrong, You Have Nothing to Hide)

IV. Fallacies of Questionable Legitimations

A. The Fallacy of Applying a War Mentality to Domestic Problems (this can suspend basic civil liberties and civil rights and dehumanize the subject)

B. The Fallacy of Failing to Value Civil Society (the failure to appreciate borders between the coercive power of government or large corporations and individuals and small groups)

C. The Fallacy of Explicit Agendas (the assumption that the goals are clear)

D. The Legalistic Fallacy That Just Because You Have a Legal Right to Do Something, It Is the Right Thing to Do (subordinates morality to the procedure of passing a law)

E. The Fallacy of Single-Value or goal Primacy (not seeing the presence of multiple goals and values)

F. The Fallacy of Lowest-Common-Denominator Morality

G. The Fallacy That the Experts (or Their Creations) Always Know What Is Best

H. The Fallacy of the Velvet Glove (if it is soft and manipulative rather than directly coercive it is therefore acceptable)

I. The Fallacy That If It Is New, It Is Better (the old ways, even with their limits, should not automatically be replaced by a new method)

J. The Fallacy That Because Civil Liberties and Civil Rights Are Historically Recent and Extend to Only a Fraction of the World's Population, They Can't Be Very Important

K. The Fallacy of the Legitimation via Transference (endorsement of a solution by a well-known person who is not an expert)

V. Fallacies of Logical or Empirical Analysis

    A. The Fallacy of Acontextuality (failing to appreciate the importance of the local context or setting)

    B. The Fallacy of Reductionism (offering an explanation that attributes cause to a single factor)

    C. The Fallacy of a Bygone Golden Age Where There Were No Such Problems

    D. The Fallacy That Correlation Must Equal Causality (instead some additional factor may be responsible for what is a spurious correlation)

    E. The Fallacy of the Short Run

    F. The Fallacy That Greater Expenditures and More Powerful and Faster Technology Will Continually Yield Benefits in a Linear Fashion (a gradient fallacy—if some is good, more is better)

    G. The Fallacy That Demand Not Supply Causes A Social Problem (they interact)

    H. The Fallacy That Because It Is Possible to Successfully Skate on Thin Ice, It Is Wise to Do So (here we also see the response to a negative scenario suggested by a critic, "but that's never happened," to which the critic can respond, "No, it hasn't happened yet."

    I. The Fallacy of Rearranging the Deck Chairs on the Titanic instead of Looking for Icebergs.

The ethical aspects can be further drawn out by asking the following questions of a given solution.

Questions for the Ethics of Social Problem Solutions

1. Initial Conditions: Policies, Procedures, and Capabilities

Formal procedure and public input in the decision to adopt: Does the decision to apply a social problems solution grow out of an established, participatory review procedure?

Role reversal: Would those applying the solution agree to be its subjects if roles were reversed? How would the agents who are now in the role of subjects view efforts to neutralize surveillance?

Restoration: Does the proposed technique radically break with traditional expectations about how individuals are to be treated?

Unwanted precedents: Is the solution likely to create precedents that will lead to its application in undesirable ways?

Symbolic meaning: Does the solution and the way it is applied communicate a respectful view of citizens who have rights that is appropriate for a democratic society?

Reversibility: If experience suggests that the policy is undesirable, how easily can the means be given up in the face of large capital expenditures and vested interests backing the status quo?

Written policies: Does an agency have policies to guide use of the tactic, and are these periodically reviewed?

Agency competence and resources: Does the organization have the resources, skills, and motivation to appropriately and effectively apply, interpret, and use the tactic?

2. Means

Validity: Are there publicly offered grounds for concluding that the tactic in general (and as applied in specific cases) is valid, and is it periodically checked?

Human review: Is there human review of machine-generated results—both basic data and (if present) automated recommendations for action?

Alternative means: Is this the best available means? How does it compare to other means with respect to ease of application, validity, costs, risks, and measuring outcomes? Is there a tilt toward counting (in both senses) what can most easily and inexpensively be measured, rather than toward what is more directly linked to the goal?

3. Goals

Clarity and appropriateness of goals: Are the goals clearly stated, justified, and (if more than one) prioritized?

4. Connections between Means and Goals

The goodness of fit between the means and the goal: Is there a clear link between the information sought and the goal to be achieved?

Inaction as action: Where the only available tool is costly, risky, and/or weakly related to the goal because what is of interest is difficult to detect or statistically very unlikely to occur, has consideration been given to taking no action or to redefining the goal?

Proportionality: Do means and ends stand in appropriate balance?

Timeliness: Is a tactic that is initially justified still needed or has a goal been met or a problem reduced such that it is unnecessary and even unwise to continue to use it?

5. Application

Minimization: Is the tactic applied with minimum intrusiveness and invasiveness, with only the amount and kind of personal information necessary for the goal collected and analyzed? Where personal data is taken from different contexts are these kept separate?

Border crossings: Does the technique cross a sensitive and intimate personal boundary (whether bodily, relational, spatial, or symbolic) with notice and/or permission? If consent is given, is it genuine?

6. Harmful Consequences for Subjects

Harm and disadvantage: Does the intervention cause unwarranted physical, psychological, or social harm or disadvantage to the subject, the agent, or third parties?

7. Rights and Resources of Subjects

Right of inspection: Are subjects aware of the nature of the solution and its results?

Right to challenge and express a grievance: Are there procedures for challenging the results and for entering alternative data or interpretations into the record?

Redress and sanctions: If an individual or groups have been wronged, are there means of discovery and redress? And, if appropriate, for the correction or destruction of the records?

8. Consequences for Agents and Third Parties

Harm to agents: Can undesirable impacts on the values and personality of the surveillance agent be avoided?

Spillover to uninvolved third parties: Can the tactic be restricted to appropriate subjects?

A flashing yellow light—a "slow down and think" response—rather than a green or red light, is initially called for in the face of the rush to solutions. Of course, in a world on the brink, it is imperative to have a dream and venture forth. Not to do so is to be a part of the problem. Yet, while we shoot for the moon, optimism must be tempered with awareness of how sweeping ideas, enthusiastically put forth (particularly during election years!) can complicate, and sometimes weaken, the connection between good intentions and good outcomes.

Dialogue and analysis of the empirical, logical, and ethical assumptions found in discussions of social problems certainly do not guarantee just and effective outcomes, but they are surely necessary conditions.

Key Resources

Ellul, J. 1964. *The Technological Society.* New York, NY: Vintage Books.

Mander, J. 1992. *In the Absence of the Sacred: The Failure of Technology and the Survival of the Indian Nations.* San Francisco, CA: Sierra Club Books.

Marx, G.T. 2016. *Windows Into the Soul: Surveillance and Society in an Age of High Technology.* Chicago, IL: University of Chicago Press.

Mumford, Lewis. 1934. *Technics and Civilization.* London: George Routledge and Sons.

Postman, N. 1992. *Technopoly: The Surrender of Culture to Technology.* New York, NY: Knopf.

About the Author

Gary T. Marx, Ph.D. is Professor Emeritus from M.I.T. He has worked in the areas of race and ethnicity, collective behavior and social movements, law and society, and surveillance studies. He is recipient of the Surveillance Studies Network's *Outstanding Achievement Award.* He has written many books, with his most recent, *Windows into the Soul: Surveillance and Society in an Age of High Technology*, published by University of Chicago Press this year. His work has appeared or been reprinted in over 300 books, monographs, and periodicals, and has been translated into Japanese, Chinese, French, Italian, Spanish, Hebrew, Dutch, German, Russian, Polish, Hungarian, Greek, Turkish, Portuguese, Farsi, Macedonian, and other languages.

Afterword:
The Importance of Social Movements for Transformative Policy Solutions Towards Inclusive Social Justice and Democracy

Brian V. Klocke

Four years ago, in the 2012 edition of *Agenda for Social Justice,* I wrote about citizens' frustration with Federal policy-making, their "growing anger around bipartisan decisions that go against the grain of public desire," and their increasing support for policies advancing social justice. When I wrote that, many of the encampments of the Occupy Wall Street movement (OWS) had already been dismantled, but their calls for the country to address economic inequality had an impact on the 2012 election. President Obama was asked about OWS in a news conference of October 6, 2011. His response was, "I think it expresses the frustrations that the American people feel—that we had the biggest financial crisis since the Great Depression, huge collateral damage all throughout the country, all across Main Street.... the protestors are giving voice to a more broad-based frustration about how our financial system works."

We continue to see this manifested in this year's Presidential election cycle, where anti-establishment campaigns in both dominant political parties have garnered much popular support. Analysts say that the message of political and economic inequality has resonated with many voters on the left and the right who feel they have been left out and left behind in the economic recovery from the Great Recession of 2007 to 2009. Thus, many Americans believe that establishment politicians no longer represent the interests of the people. Most 2015 studies show that income and wealth inequality, indeed, have risen over the last few decades, and have continued to rise since the 2012 publication of *Agenda for Social Justice*, by some measures, to record levels.

Times when Federal policies have decreased social inequality

There are two historical periods where economic inequality and/ or poverty were significantly reduced in the United States due to an expansion of federal policies, programs, and funds investing in a social safety net: the first being in the years following Franklin Delano Roosevelt's (FDR) 'New Deal' programs implemented from 1933 to 1938 to stave off the Great Depression, and the second, in the years following Lyndon Baines Johnson's (LBJ) Great Society programs of 1964 to 1969. The New Deal directed efforts at regulating the financial system (e.g., Glass-Steagall Act), creating jobs (e.g., Civilian Conservation Corps), protecting workers (e.g., Fair Labor Standards Act), and aiding the poor and the elderly (e.g., Social Security). The enactment of these social policies, which included a national minimum wage and subsidized housing, would arguably not have been possible without decades of struggle by the labor movement. However, due to institutional discrimination, these programs disproportionately benefited white men due to a 'race-neutral' approach, which, Childers and Garcia informed us in Chapter 8 of this book, serves to "mask racism [but] not eliminate it."

LBJ, three decades later, winning a landslide election, called for an end to poverty and racial injustice, proclaiming a "War on Poverty" that went beyond FDR's New Deal. The poverty rate under President Johnson's administration fell seven points to just over 12 percent in 1969. His administration expanded health care for the elderly and the poor by creating Medicare and Medicaid, provided legal protection for minorities with passage of the Civil Rights Acts of 1964 and 1968 and the Voting Rights Acts, provided job training (e.g., Vista), made Food Stamps (now called SNAP) permanent, created Head Start for children, increased funding for higher education, offered student loans at subsidized rates, and started programs assisting low-income, first-generation and students with disabilities (now called TRiO programs). Urban redevelopment programs improving access to public transportation, housing, home ownership, and community centers in low-income areas were also initiated, as well as regulations on environmental hazards. LBJ's broad-ranging social policies happened during a time of massive social protest and urban uprisings, and wouldn't have been possible without many years of struggle by the civil rights movement and other social justice movements.

The rise of Neoliberalism and the erosion of the social safety net

LBJ warned in his 1964 University of Michigan speech that, "the Great Society is not a safe harbor... a finished work," but "a challenge [that must be] constantly renewed." In the following three decades, unheeded by the warning, neoliberalism, bolstered succeedingly by the Reagan, Bush, and Clinton administrations, became the economic orthodoxy, succeeding at deregulating global financial systems (through trade agreements, development programs, and structural adjustment programs adhered to loans), privatizing public resources, and dismantling much of what was derisively called "the nanny state." Reagan, in his first term cut taxes for the wealthy while increasing them for the poor and cut funding for social service programs (some of which he eased in his second term), facilitated many corporate mergers, and deregulated the savings and loan industry; Bush, Sr. bailed out the industry; Clinton repealed the Glass-Steagall Act, passed NAFTA (after Bush, Sr. failed), helped establish the World Trade Organization (one of the big three neoliberal financial organizations), and dismantled the federal welfare program. These anti-social welfare policies and structural changes have led to steady increases in income and wealth inequality in the U.S. and globally, as well as exacerbated racial and ethnic economic disparities, despite more than a doubling of worker productivity.

Sociologists Robert and Carolyn Perrucci presciently wrote in 2009, in their introduction to *America at Risk*, "The cumulative impact of this polarized society on the average American over the last thirty years or so has been the loss of hope for a better future, the decline in trust for our mainstream institutions, and the declining support for government programs that express help and caring for those who live on the fringes of society." Their analysis gives further explanation for the popular support of an anti-establishment campaign in the Republican party, as well as in the Democratic party, the latter of which seems to be more about the Perruccis' call for restoring trust, caring, and hope.

The creation of the global neoliberal economy, favoring large corporations and the wealthy at the expense of the poor and working class, has been described by sociologists as "corporate welfare," and by many others—most famously Herbert Gans in a 1995 book of the same name—as a *War Against the Poor*. Since 2003, the national poverty rate has been above the 12.1 percent rate achieved in 1969. The latest figures from the Census Bureau (2014) report it is now 14.8 percent with 46.7 million people living in poverty. However, for blacks, the poverty rate has always been much higher than the country's average rate. In 1966 it was a whopping 41.8 percent, dropping to 32.5 percent in 1969, reaching its lowest rate on record of 22.5 percent in 2000, but increasing to 26.2 percent in post-recession 2014, with Hispanics/Latinos at a close 23.6 percent. Former SSSP President Anna Santiago's 2014 address, titled "Fifty Years Later: From a War on Poverty to a War on the Poor," gave evidence "that poverty rates today would be significantly higher had we not had the safety net in place at all."

Effective social policies require comprehensive systemic and structural change addressing social inequalities

The extent to which LBJ's War on Poverty was successful was due to its comprehensive and systematic approach of repairing holes in the social safety net, by addressing education, jobs, hunger, health care, housing, transportation, environmental pollution, immigration (albeit very limitedly), discrimination, and voting rights. Yet importantly, as the authors in this book have addressed persuasively through their summation of the best available research evidence available, we as a country have much more to do for all of us to "get to the promised land," as Martin Luther King, Jr. (MLK), prophesied the night before he was assassinated in April, 1968. Civil rights, human rights, immigrant rights, and environmental justice, as discussed in previous chapters of this book, are all important social issues our country still faces in 2016. Missing from this list are two more important issues that both FDR and LBJ did not attempt a solution for: the problem of mass incarceration and inequality within the criminal justice system, which is covered in this book, and the other, which is not covered, that of militarism and war, which compounds poverty by drawing federal resources that could go towards social programs, and by the costly medical expenses of mentally and/or physically wounded soldiers, as well as family income lost to death.

Ironically, LBJ, despite his often cordial private relationship with MLK on social issues, did not agree with the Kerner Commission's famous 1968 report (released before MLK's death) that our nation was "moving toward two societies, one black, one white—separate and unequal." He rejected their recommendations—some of which would have created more integrated neighborhoods—and is reported to have thought that they were too radical. However, this aligns with his pre-1957, segregationist Congressional voting record reported by historian Robert Caro. Months prior to LBJ's 1964 election, an incident happened where a white off-duty police officer in New York City shot and killed a 15-year-old African American boy, sparking thousands of Harlem residents to rebel in the streets, setting the stage for uprisings in six more cities before the end of the year and many more through the end of the decade.

Social movements are a necessary part of democracy and the creation of social justice

Two similar situations occurred in February of 2012 in Sanford, Florida, and August of 2014, in Ferguson, Missouri. In Sanford, a self-appointed Neighborhood Watch man shot and killed teenager Trayvon Martin, leading to nationwide protests in July of 2013 after his killer was acquitted, and three black queer women to spontaneously create #blacklivesmatter, which formed into a social network movement over the next year as more black victims died at the hands of police and others. It grew much larger when a Ferguson on-duty police officer shot and killed African American teenager Michael Brown, and a grand jury investigation failed to indict his killer, sparking months of protest and a continual building of the movement as similar incidents keep happening each year.

Just as the Occupy Wall Street Movement which sprung up in 2011 impacted the 2012 Presidential election, making it easier for the failed candidate Mitt Romney to be depicted as an out-of-touch member of the 1% who had disdain for the poor, activists who identify with the Black Lives Matter (BLM) movement have already had an influence on the 2016 Presidential primary process. They have, among other things, confronted candidates at campaign rallies and events, forcing them to talk more directly about racial inequality, police abuse, and criminal justice system reform. Additionally, at least one BLM activist is running for political office as a mayoral candidate of a major city, releasing a wide-ranging policy platform with specifics of how he would address social inequality in education, employment, wages, affordable housing and homeownership, criminal justice, environmental justice, health care, and more. OWS' theme of contrasting inequality between the wealthy 1 percent and the struggling 99 percent of the population has also made its way into the campaign discourse of at least one 2016 Presidential candidate, and BLM groups and the issues they raise will certainly impact the political process and elections beyond this year.

However, will we, in another four years be back to talking about these same persistent issues of structural inequalities and social injustice, or will social movements and social unrest succeed in creating more immediate and much needed transformative change? There are some ripples of hope, such as recent success in the Fight For $15 movement that has seen several cities and now a couple of states agree to raising the minimum wage to $15 per hour over a few years, as well as promises from one Presidential candidate to raise the national minimum wage to $15 per hour and another to $12, both with additional promises to address social inequality, if elected. While significant, it is doubtful that these increased wages will truly be a living wage for working families at the time of their implementation. More systemic change is needed to transform politics and policies that as usual have not ended the rise in income and wealth inequality, which hinders solutions to many other important social issues raised in this book.

In order to create the political will and understanding for systemic social policy changes, we need not only to create public education campaigns and identify empathetic governmental officials and who are allies, but as many of the contributors of this book have indicated, to also have social movements, as a part of the solution, to agitate and advocate for social justice. We do need federal policies in the U.S. that set national community standards so that every local community will be required to uphold the democratic human rights of individuals and the collective rights of social groups, as well as the sustainability of our planet. However, federal policies and programs, in themselves, are not enough to create solutions to social inequalities, even with the pressure from social movements. Policies, programs, organizations, and social movements that work to transform structures and dynamics of power at the interpersonal, cultural, institutional, national, and global levels, will have the most long-term success at eradicating social inequality and bringing about human rights, collective rights, and community-based social justice.

Inclusive social movements that address multiple, interrelated issues of social inequality and social justice are a crucial component of creating remedies to persistent social problems. The People's Institute for Survival and Beyond remind us that "People are not poor because they lack programs and services; people are poor because they lack power." Social justice-based policy solutions require a shift in the dynamics of power that have created the social problems being addressed. Thus, the people that policies and programs are meant to serve must be included in the leadership directing the design and implementation of them, as well as provided access to resources to make it happen, without cooptation to the agendas of privileged groups, if the solutions are to be systemically effective and sustainable.

In essence, this is what social justice and democracy—rule by the people—looks like. And it takes all of us to get there. As the motto of the 2016 World Social Forum boldly declares, "Another world is needed. Together it is Possible!"

Key Resources

Albo, Gregory. 2001. "Neoliberalism from Reagan to Clinton." *Monthly Review*, 52(11): 81-89.

Black Lives Matter http://blacklivesmatter.com

Census Bureau Historical Poverty Tables. Retrieved April 7, 2016. https://www.census.gov/hhes/www/poverty/data/historical/people.html

Fight for $15. Retrieved April 7, 2016. http://fightfor15.org

Fry, Richard and Rakesh Kochhar. 2014. "America's Wealth Gap Between Middle-income and Upper-income Families is Widest on Record." Retrieved April 7, 2016. http://www.pewresearch.org/fact-tank/2014/12/17/wealth-gap-upper-middle-income/

Gans, Herbert J. 1995. *The War Against The Poor: The Underclass And Antipoverty Policy*. New York, NY: Basic Books.

Miller Center of Public Affairs, University of Virginia. "Lyndon B. Johnson: Domestic Affairs." Retrieved April 7, 2016. http://millercenter.org/president/biography/lbjohnson-domestic-affairs.

Occupy Wall Street http://occupywallstreet.net/learn

Perrucci, Robert and Carolyn C. Perrucci. 2009. *America at Risk: The Crisis of Hope, Trust, and Caring*. Lanham, MD: Rowman and Littlefield.

Santiago, Anna Maria. 2015. "Fifty Years Later: From a War on Poverty to a War on the Poor." *Social Problems*, 62: 2-14.

World Social Forum. Retrieved April 7, 2016. https://fsm2016.org/en/

About the Author

Brian V. Klocke, Ph.D. is an independent scholar, educator, journalist, and photographer. His collaborative and singular research on social movements, moral panic, masculinities, and media framing has appeared in the journals *Journalism Studies, Journalism, Sociology Compass, Policing and Society*, and *Men and Masculinities*, and in the books *Lost in Media: The Ethics of Everyday Life*, and *The Ashgate Research Companion to Moral Panics*. He is co-author of *The Better World Handbook: From Good*

Intentions to Everyday Actions (1st Ed.), and has a chapter in *Sociologists in Action on Inequalities: Race, Class, Gender, and Sexuality*. He is also a member of the leadership team of Faculty Against Rape (http://www. facultyagainstrape.net).